MW00578438

ISLAND MEDICINE

Life, Healing, and Community on a Maine Island

To Ship !

CHUCK RADIS

Chuck Radis MD—

Down East Books

Camden, Maine

Down East Books

Published by Down East Books
An imprint of Globe Pequot
Trade division of The Rowman & Littlefield Publishing Group, Inc.
4501 Forbes Boulevard, Suite 200, Lanham, Maryland 20706
www.rowman.com

Distributed by NATIONAL BOOK NETWORK

Library of Congress Cataloging-in-Publication Data on File
ISBN 978-1-60893-746-2 (cloth : alk. paper)
ISBN 978-1-68475-018-4 (electronic)

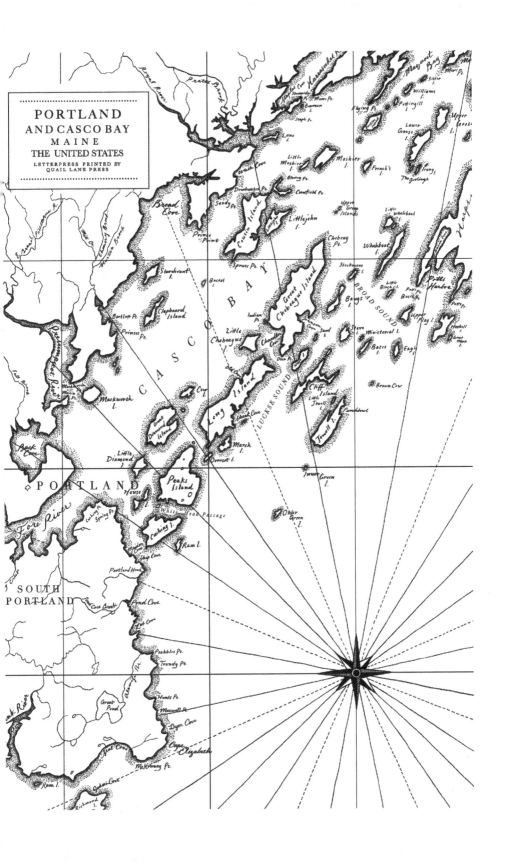

PORTLAND
AND CASCO BAY
MAINE
THE UNITED STATES
LETTERPRESS PRINTED BY
QUAIL LANE PRESS

ACKNOWLEDGMENTS

To Betsy Gattis and Geoff Gattis, your gift of friendship to our family is sorely missed. To my agent, Jeanne Fredericks, I am grateful you asked me if I had another book in mind when you turned down the first. Your steady encouragement and expert guidance gave me confidence to keep persevering.

To my wife, Sandi: Thank you for allowing me to share both our struggles and successes during these past 43 years of marriage. Without you, there wouldn't be a story. Or, as one reader commented on an early draft, "I want to hear more about Sandi; she's a lot more interesting than you."

AUTHOR'S NOTE

Though the stories I present are true, the patients in *Island Medicine* are blended, to protect individual patient's privacy.

I flipped off the headlights of my truck on Widgery Wharf and clicked my neck, first to the right, then more forcibly to the left. Another missed ferry. A half-eaten chicken salad sandwich and an unopened Snickers bar lay within arm's reach on the passenger seat. A stethoscope and six patient charts from my afternoon clinic on Chebeague Island protruded from my green satchel. My beeper vibrated. 766-5915. That would be home.

It was 1989. A phone booth stood at the far end of the wharf beneath a street light. The only person I knew with a cellular phone was my friend Jim. His phone took up a third of the space in his briefcase. When he needed to make a call, he pulled over and placed a specialized antenna with a suction cup on his car roof before dialing. His phone cost nearly $2,000. That's a lot of quarters. Gulping down the remnants of the sandwich, I stuffed the Snickers into the front pocket of my windbreaker, zipped up the satchel, and headed for the phone booth.

My boots crunched against a thin rim of ice where the afternoon's rain pooled on the rutted wharf. A brisk, raw wind flushed dried leaves, light gravel, and empty beer cans off the end of the wharf into Casco Bay. I thumbed through the pockets of my windbreaker, hoping to find a knit cap or gloves and remembered exactly where they were: at home, in the kitchen closet, stuffed in the pocket of my parka, the parka my wife Sandi reminded me to wear today because most people change into more sensible clothes when the temperature dips into the teens. When I deposited a quarter into the coin slot, I heard a hollow metallic clink, then a dial tone. I exhaled and felt my neck and shoulders relax. At least I was out of the wind.

"Hi Sandra." In the background I could hear jumping and squealing. Kate, age five was challenging her sister, Molly, nearly 2, to jump from the landing of the stairs into a jungle pit of friendly snakes.

"Hello my mate. Missed the 5:35 ferry?" Her voice was even, unhurried, even if she *was* monitoring controlled chaos. I imagined her looking up at the clock above the closet. If the closet was open, she might even notice my parka, neatly hung on a hook, with knit cap and mittens sticking out of the pockets.

"I hit some traffic coming down Commercial Street and just now pulled into Widgery Wharf," I explained.

"I know you try," her voice trailed off, "but this is the third 5:35 ferry you've missed this week." It wasn't an accusation, merely a statement of fact. "The next ferry doesn't leave Portland until 7:15, and by the time you walk home it'll be after 8:00. I'll need to put Molly to bed before you arrive. She'll be . . ."

"Hey, Sandra," I interrupted, "I'm in luck. A police cruiser just pulled into the lot. It's Officer Mike and Big John. I bet they're heading for the police boat down by the fish pier. If I hurry, I can catch a ride on the *Connolly* to Peaks and be home in thirty minutes. Lucky me. Love you."

Heading off at a lope, I caught the pair as they clambered down the iron ladder from the wharf to the float where the police boat was cleated. Mike, short and solid as a fire hydrant, descended first; Big John, his crewcut exposing a pair of outsized ears, lowered himself two rungs at a time, the iron ladder swaying under his weight. A sprinkling of ice from my boots peppered John's head. He released a hand and looked up, shielding his head from the debris, and grinned, "Doctor Radis, great night for a boat ride."

I snugged up my jacket and followed Mike and John down the ladder. I am of average height, trim, with bowed legs and a brushy mustache. My hair, a tawny light brown and prematurely thinned, had not seen a barber since Mr. Sherris took off a bit around the ears for my high school yearbook photo. Ever since we met at Bates College, Sandi has trimmed my hair with a Manning and Bowman Haircut Kit, the same kit her mother used to cut Sandi's hair on the dairy farm she grew up on.

My teeth are—charitably—yellowed. If you looked closely, you'd see a ragged line in the upper front incisors from a baseball bat flung backwards by a ten-year-old boy who connected unexpectedly with a pitched ball. Afterward, the dentist pulled the teeth down from the roof of my mouth and suggested I move from catcher to right field.

I never wear a white coat. I don't own a suit. Because I abhor shopping, Sandi (gladly) purchases most of my clothes, often at second-hand stores. This is one of her joys in life, finding bargains. I guess one might say that I have a personal shopper. A keen observer would say that I am in assisted care.

Although the *Connolly* was more than thirty feet long and heavy-beamed, a wave suddenly lifted the bow and slammed it against the oversized fenders holding it off the dock. Bulky chains creaked and groaned as the dock rode up and down against a pair of pilings the size of telephone poles.

After Mike and Big John boarded the *Connolly* and stowed their gear, Mike motioned me inside and closed the door of the pilot house. "It may be a few minutes. They need to pull one of the lieutenants off the front desk up town so we have someone to captain the boat again tonight." Mike methodically checked the navigational lights and bilge pump and flipped on the radar and heater before reaching up overhead for a spare key taped inside a navigational chart. The engine turned over and idled smoothly.

"I hope it's not Lieutenant Benton," Big John said, warming his hands over the heater. "I hear the guy managed to blow an engine off Fort Gorges a couple of months ago and they had to drop anchor and wait for the Coast Guard to tow the *Connolly* back to town. Jerk."

I raised an eyebrow. "Let me try to understand this," I said as I stored my backpack and satchel under the console. "You and Mike both have your own boats and lobster in your spare time, right?" John nodded and handed me a life jacket as he zipped up his own. "So why don't one of you captain the boat?"

"Because," Mike glared, turning back to me, "Because a lieutenant needs to pilot the boat. That's our orders."

"Oh," I smiled. Delicate topic.

There was a tap on the window. A pasty faced, plump man in a white parka, wearing penny loafers, police trousers with a side holster, and a pair of arctic mittens stared back at me. "Gentlemen! It's a hell of a night! Should I get the lines?" he shouted above the wind.

"No sir. You're piloting the boat sir. I'll get the lines." Big John exchanged places with the lieutenant and stood motionless on the dock, awaiting further instructions. Inside the dimly lit cabin, lieutenant Benton produced a key attached to a miniature red foam buoy from his zippered front pocket, and attempted, unsuccessfully, to force it into the ignition. There seemed to be something blocking access. He sat down in the pilot seat and tried again. It was Mike who explained that it was awfully dark in the pilot house, but that there was already a key in the ignition. The engine was running. He and John wanted to make sure the *Connolly* was running smoothly before heading across the bay.

"Of course," Lieutenant Benton said stiffly. "Makes sense. Good work," he added.

"Are you ready sir?" Big John undid the bow and stern lines and held the *Connolly* off against the wind. "I need to give her a push to clear the dock, otherwise we're going to grind against the pilings," he shouted, then mumbled, "Like we did last time."

Officer Benton clutched the wheel. John pushed off against the wheelhouse, separating the boat from the dock. "Now!" Big John yelled. The lieutenant thrust the throttle forward and the *Connolly* lurched away, Big John just barely grabbing a side rail as he jumped on board. For a big man he was agile as a cat.

Underway, Lieutenant Benton turned the bow toward the islands of Casco Bay, the compass on the console swinging around to 85 degrees, a straight shot to the first green blinking navigational can a mile distant. I was lulled into a measure of comfort; the *Connolly* had the wind and following seas at her back, and the lieutenant poured himself a half cup of coffee from a thermos as he concentrated on the radar screen. Three miles distant a faint cluster of lights marked the wharf on Peaks Island.

Late October is an unpredictable time on Casco Bay. By mid-month, pleasure boats are on jack stands in boatyards or driveways, winterized and shrink-wrapped, awaiting spring. Lobster traps are pulled and stacked; seal and whale watching tour boats motor south to winter tourist areas. A few larger lobster boats and trawlers still ply the deeper offshore waters, but the work can be brutal; gale-force winds and heavy snow may blanket Casco Bay one day, and the next, a warm breeze might flutter in from the south with temperatures in the sixties.

The bay cools slowly. Topping out at about 64 degrees in mid-summer, by January the water hovers just above freezing. Every five or ten years, the inner bay, at least around the Portland waterfront, freezes solid. Every twenty or thirty years, ice extends as far as Peaks Island. Looking out from the *Connolly*, I figured I'd last ten, maybe fifteen minutes tonight if I fell overboard, that is, if I didn't cramp up or panic.

Lieutenant Benton's nose pressed up against the radar screen, his parka's tunneled hood obscuring his face. We passed an ocean tugboat pushing a barge toward Merrill's Marine Terminal up the Fore River. A flock of seagulls flushed from where they rested on the water. The trawler *Northern Lights* unloaded its catch at the Custom House Wharf. Three spotlights illuminated the deck while a hose suctioned up thousands of pounds of herring from the hold. Lieutenant Benton pushed the throttle forward and the *Connolly* accelerated through the rolling black seas. A loon, panicking, rose up and dove for cover. I reached out and grabbed the console for support. We came over the top of one wave and bounced heavily into the trough and I noticed that the deck was awash in coffee.

"Lieutenant," Mike peered through the windshield. "We're coming up on the Number 5 green can."

"I know. I can see it clearly on the radar."

"Lieutenant!" Mike repeated. "We're dead on."

"I know," the lieutenant answered,a note of irritation in his voice. "I can see exactly. . ." Abruptly his head bobbed up from the screen. The green, one-ton blinking Number 5 navigational can loomed directly ahead. He swung the wheel sharply, but in his panic neglected to throttle back. The bow of the *Connolly* nearly clipped the can. I fell off my seat. Big John banged his head on the low ceiling of the cabin. Mike, legs firmly planted apart, glowered at the back of the lieutenant.

"That came up fast," Lieutenant Benton muttered as he stroked his pencil thin mustache. On we sped toward Peaks Island. The gray silhouette of Fort Gorges—an old Civil War fortification—rose up on our port side, shouldered by breaking waves churning over a shallow ledge extending east and west. We're a good hundred yards outside the blinking red buoy, safely away from the shoals. Through the gunnery openings I noticed a flickering, orange glow.

Big John pointed to the pale outlines of a skiff pulled up on the sand beach. "Party Island, Doc. Some group of yahoos is camping somewhere inside. They probably have a bonfire going in the courtyard. I hope they have their skiff squared away and don't get too drunk. The last thing I want to do is rescue some idiot with a broken leg later tonight. And don't think we won't call you for help," John smirked.

I peered past Fort Gorges down Diamond Pass—the channel separating the Diamond Islands from Peaks Island—and spied a pair of red and green navigational lights plowing through the waves. Probably a lobster boat from Long Island down the bay, I decided, or maybe even a vessel from Chebeague or Cliff Island bucking the headwinds to drop off their catch in Portland. The sight of the lobster boat triggered something else. That's the problem with running clinics on both Peaks and Chebeague islands, daily hospital rounds, and a part-time in-town practice, I had an uneasy feeling there was something I promised to do tomorrow and neglected to write down; a phone call, maybe a request or favor. I closed my eyes and focused. Something I needed to do tomorrow. Something. I pulled my 3-by-5-inch At-a-Glance pocket calendar from my shirt pocket and clicked my ballpoint pen. There. Now I remembered, and scribbled, *House call Cliff Island, Yohanna Von-Tiling* and then: *Hat/Gloves.*

Officer Mike tapped his commanding officer on the shoulder. The outline of Peaks loomed ahead in the darkness, the wharf coming into sharp relief. On the north side of the wharf, a metal ramp angled down to the public safety float. "Lieutenant, we're coming up on Peaks."

"I can see it on the screen. I'm heading for the public safety float," Lieutenant Benton replied.

"Sir, you're coming in too fast."

A Jeep pulled up on the wharf, its headlights bouncing off the water. We flew by Rick Crowley's scallop boat, *E. Cosi,* and Bobby Emerson's lobster boat, the *Grammie Annie,* nodding on their moorings. The lieutenant pulled back ever so slightly on the throttle, his face still glued to the hypnotizing game being played out on the radar screen.

Big John whispered in my ear, "Grab your stuff, *now*. This guy is a major jerk." Two figures on the wharf emerged from the jeep and waved the *Connolly* off. We were coming in hot. Reflexively, I grabbed my backpack and satchel and scrambled after Mike and John outside the pilot house. For a moment I didn't quite understand what Big John had in mind. Then he leaned into my ear and shouted, "When I count to three, jump onto the public safety float!"

Wait. That was the plan? Jump? I blinked and tried to make sense of our predicament. Dead on, not thirty feet beyond the public safety float, was Covey's Lobster Shack. On the waterside of Covey's, was a finger pier with lobster traps neatly stacked on one end and a dinghy tied on the other. Oh my.

"One." Mike and John crouched on the rail of the *Connolly*. "Two." I reluctantly joined them.

"Three!"

At the moment we jumped, Lieutenant Benton, in a panic, abruptly threw the *Connolly* into full reverse. We tumbled onto the public safety float, rolling toward the opposite edge. Big John reached out and caught my leg. I felt a sudden, unwelcome tearing sensation in both shins. We sprung upright. The *Connolly* lurched to a full-on stop, the back-wake surging over the float nearly knocking us over as the boat settled in the water.

Lieutenant Benton stuck his head out the pilot window. "You guys are crazy! There was no need to jump!" Above the howling wind I heard a tinny, metallic, grinding noise. A puff of smoke rose from the diesel cowling. A darker cloud followed. "Wait! I need help tying off!" the lieutenant shouted. Big John and Mike, pretending not to hear, silently trudged up the ramp. Somehow, I'd held on to my satchel and backpack.

The two men on the wharf who tried to wave us off were police officers. I stood off to one side and listened as Mike and Big John received their shift report, the wind whipping off the water, knit caps pulled over their ears. Now and then, Big John, looming over the others, glowered in the general direction of the *Connolly*. The report was routine. Major crime is almost unheard of on Peaks Island, but during the summer months—when the population may swell from 850 year-round islanders to 3,000 visitors—public intoxication, loose dogs, fights, and neighbor disputes require police intervention, and an occasional arrest. We are not immune to domestic abuse, which is often alcohol fueled or, in more recent years, connected to drug use. Fortunately, fire, which places the entire island at risk, is exceedingly rare. Older islanders still remember the Great Fire of 1948, when three-fourths of Peaks burned after a fire broke out on the old military reservation, barely sparing most of the year-round community and businesses clustered near the ferry dock.

We're fortunate to have a group of patrolmen who enjoy the slower pace of island police work. What's more, in an age of specialization, the police on Peaks are triple-trained: each officer has fire-fighting capabilities and is a certified EMT (emergency medical technician.) Peaks Island, along with House, Cushing, Little and Great Diamond, Long and Cliff Islands, are distinct cultural neighborhoods of the city of Portland. Our property taxes pay the salaries of our police, the librarian, teachers at our elementary school, and our public safety workers, which is good or bad, depending on who you talk with. Me, I like local control; I want to secede and form our own town. Sandi wants to stick with Portland.

Mike and Big John offered to drive me home. The off-duty patrolmen on the wharf tossed their cigarettes into the bay and marched down the ramp, their backs bent and forlorn, awaiting further orders.

Big John turned the Jeep around as Mike rubbed his hands over the heat vent and I crammed into the front seat. A pool of water formed on the floorboards. The adrenaline rush of our jump was dissipating, replaced by a deep aching in my lower legs and left hip. It was Big John who snorted first, trying unsuccessfully to stifle a laugh. Officer Mike erupted in a high pitched, staccato titter. Shivering uncontrollably, I joined in.

As the Jeep worked its way up the cobblestones of Welch Street, we passed Jones Landing, a restaurant and bar. I remembered my first visit to Peaks Island five years ago to explore the possibilities of an island medical practice. I was at Jones Landing, sitting at the bar waiting for the ferry, when an anchored sailboat exploded into flames not fifty yards off shore. The flames triggered a lively conversation at the bar. No one seemed particularly concerned other than to note that the owner wasn't on board—and that he was an idiot.

Midway up the hill was Lisa's Peaks Island Café. A few minutes before the early morning ferries is a delicate time in the cafe. Islanders want to fill their mugs, pay their bills, and rush down the hill to make the ferry. Woe to someone who cuts the line. Without a word, Lisa may famously dump your coffee in the sink or allow your egg sandwich to drop onto the floor. If you value your health, don't cross Lisa. She brews your coffee.

Danger lurked outside Lisa's as well. The hill is short but steep. I had patients with emphysema or heart disease who could barely navigate the hill. If I was coming off the ferry behind them, I casually observed their progress. If they paused at the stone wall in front of Lisa's, breathless—or worse, clutching their chest—I'd sidle up to them and ask, "This hill gets steeper every year, doesn't it? Here, sit down at the picnic table." A quick evaluation followed. If a few puffs on an inhaler or a tablet of nitroglycerine—I carry both in my satchel—failed to resolve the symptoms, I arranged for a transfer to Portland on the fireboat—our island rescue boat. That is, if they're willing to go. Following medical advice on Peaks Island is not a given.

The hill has other dangers. I don't know how many times I've watched islanders slip and fall on a patch of ice as they raced for the ferry. The results ran the gamut from simple stuff like sprained ankles and wrists, forearm abrasions, a bump on the head to serious injuries such as a broken hip, a fractured leg, or a concussion. For those racing downhill, I've nicknamed Welch Street the hill of mechanical mishaps, trudging uphill, heartbreak hill.

On level ground now, thirty feet above high tide, passing through the island's business section—nicknamed down front, as in, *I am going down front to pick up some milk*—we drove slowly past the candy store, the Umbrella Cover Museum, and the post office. At Feeney's Island Market, Heather, a British transplant who is married to Paul, our island plumber, worked the cash register and mysteriously tracked how much beer or liquor you recently purchased. If it's by the half gallon "for a friend" there is an informal labeling of your alcohol intake, ranging from a barely raised eyebrow to a flat-out denial of purchase. When

Jimmy Flourney staggered into Feeney's last week and managed to wiggle a case of Budweiser out of the cold case, but couldn't remain upright and pushed the case to the register on all fours, leading with his nose, Heather calmly confiscated the beer and instructed Jimmy to keep crawling out the door.

Next to Feeney's Market, is the Cockeyed Gull, our only year-round restaurant. On my way to an early morning ferry it wasn't unusual to see several islanders at the bar by the register sipping Bloody Marys or downing shots of tequila. In fact, my very first patient at the Peaks Island Health Center four years ago was a man I observed sharing a drink at the Gull with his dog Skippy. If it sounds like there's a lot of drinking on Peaks Island, it's because there is, , including on the ferry to and from Portland where passengers regularly sip their beverages from brown bags.

Above the bar, a framed photo from the 1950s shows the Peaks Island ferry off-loading passengers down a ramp onto the ice several hundred yards from shore. In the photo, mothers grasp children's hands and men in burly overcoats trudge miserably across the ice toward Peaks. Someone has taken a black magic marker and circled a barrel-chested, white-bearded man smoking a pipe and wearing a captain's cap. His pink, beefy hands are visible below the cuffs of his seaman's jacket, which is flung wide open. Above the figure is the notation. "Bud Perry"—my second patient at the Peaks Island Health Center.

Bud's gone now, his life not unlike a stream cascading down a mountainside with a series of abrupt drops, each signifying a life-threatening medical event. Each time I thought a hospitalization would lead to his demise, whether it was amputation of several toes from gangrene, pneumonia, or kidney failure requiring dialysis, he stabilized in a quiet pool, regained his caustic edge, and irritated most everyone he came in contact with—until he entered the rapids and dropped over another ledge. In his last three years, Bud visited me at the Health Center twenty-seven times. When he died, I lost a good friend. He was 71.

A blast of wind coming off City Point rocked the Jeep. Sleet peppered the windshield. Big John drove on in silence, turning left at the Peaks Island Grammar School. We slowed as a herd of deer ambled across the road in front of the Jeep. Three-quarters of a mile from the ferry, Big John pulled over and I gathered up my satchel and backpack and limped down the boardwalk toward my house.

I slipped off my shoes in the mud room without flipping on the light. Entering the kitchen, I shouted hello and turned on the stove to heat water for a cup of tea. Sandi came around the corner and her jaw dropped. A trail of blood-caked footprints followed me from the door. I looked down and realized that the front of my dress pants was torn and a burgundy red stain flowed from matching shin abrasions into my socks. So that was the tear I felt as I rolled onto the dock. I reached up and realized my pocket calendar was missing, and my pen.

Sandi grew up on a dairy farm and has a round Scandinavian face, blue eyes, long athletic legs, and blond hair that has evolved in recent years from a flowing ponytail to a shorter bob. She is matter of fact about blood, crying children, and minor injuries. In high school she was crowned Upper Valley Sewing Bee Queen and played take-no-prisoners field hockey. As a member of the local 4-H Club, she fed and groomed juvenile cows for the local county fairs. Blue ribbon or not, when a cow's days of giving milk were over, Sandi's father took the animal to the local meat cutter, and the cow transformed from a steady source of milk into dinner for the family.

Kate and Molly came roaring around the corner and stopped abruptly. Kate asked, "Daddy, is that blood?" Molly stared curiously but didn't appear particularly upset. True, her father looked scary, but he was smiling like the blood was, well, normal. Kate looked at Sandi, near tears. I felt I needed to say something, anything, so I went with, "I'm fine. Give me a minute and I'll be good as new." Kate wrapped her arm around her younger sister and disappeared back into the living room.

Under Sandi's critical eye, I stripped down in the bathroom and cleaned up the wounds. Similar to scalp wounds that bleed like stink, the cuts on the lower legs were not particularly serious. Both shins were scraped to the bone. The outer edge of my right lower calf was torn; but would close with a few Steri-Strips. I probably needed a tetanus shot. I stepped into the shower, the steaming water flowing over me. Sandi joined me to be sure that I was mostly okay. She found several additional injuries and wondered if I had broken a rib. "There's nothing to do about that, is there?" Then she told me she had an extra pocket calendar for me, just in case I lost the first one. Like most of the articles of clothing and personal items Sandi buys for me, they are bought in duplicate. "Look beneath your socks, second drawer on the right, next to a spare wallet."

Afterward, before bed, I washed down several Tylenol with a glass of water. Then I laid out my clothes for the morning and cracked open the new weekly planner to October 21st, wrote, *House call Cliff Island, Yohanna VonTiling* and added: *Hat/Gloves and flicked off the light.*

2

The phone rang. It was the answering service forwarding a patient's number. By the clock, I'd been in bed two hours. I crept down the stairs with my clothes and dialed the number. My legs throbbed. I reached for the bottle of Tylenol above the sink. A woman's voice came on the line, her breathing coming in irregular, panting gasps. "Dr. Radis, this is Liz Smith, I'm sorry for calling you so late, but I'm not sure if I'm in labor. I'm having contractions. I've been timing them and sometimes they're every two minutes and sometimes they're every five minutes. I'm not sure what to do."

I listened, quietly tapping my fingers, uneasy, hyper aware. I absolutely didn't want to deliver a baby on Peaks Island. Never mind that most babies all but deliver themselves. It is the problem deliveries, the breech births, the babies who come out unexpectedly gray and limp, the post-partum hemorrhaging, that scares the bejesus out of me. During my last year of residency, when I knew that I was going to practice on the Casco Bay islands, I scheduled several electives in pediatrics—unheard of for an internal medicine resident—but drew the line on obstetrics. No, I was not going to deliver a baby at home on Peaks Island.

The clincher came a few months before we moved to Peaks Island. I learned that a woman chose to deliver her baby at home on Peaks and something went dreadfully wrong. The baby died.

I looked down at my notes—Liz Smith was reaching out for advice. She sounded reasonable. She wanted to do the right thing. And by my own philosophy of patient care, though I had never met her before, because we were talking, she was now my patient. I couldn't, in good conscience, fob her off on the police. What if Mike and Big John had to manage the delivery as an emergency? What if it all went dreadfully wrong—and I wasn't there?

I scribbled down the address and told her I'd be right over.

13

Upstairs, I gathered up my emergency supplies from the closet shelf and reached under the bed for the pediatric endotracheal kit I had purchased several years before when a family moved to the island with a two-week-old baby with a congenital heart defect associated with Down's syndrome. By placing the kit in my emergency bag, I convinced myself I would not need to use it. Even so, I don't know how many times I'd held the tiny instrument in my hand, wondering if I could both relax and concentrate sufficiently to slide the tube down a newborn's windpipe in an emergency.

Sandi stirred. "What time is it?"

I patted her on the hip. "Midnight. I've got to see a woman in labor. I'll be back as soon as I can."

"You're limping. Take an extra Tylenol. Your parka and gloves are in the closet."

Before leaving the house, I called the police station. No answer. I scraped off a layer of ice from the windshield of our Toyota truck, and started it up. The truck was a big step up from our original vehicle on Peaks. That car, purchased for $500 from friends on the mainland when it could no longer pass inspection, was demolished when an islander plowed into it after an evening of downing shots at the Legion Hall. He hit the parked vehicle so hard, the impact sent it across the road into a snowdrift. Our new/old truck, except for the rusted floorboards, was perfect. It started in frigid weather and had good traction in the snow. The replacement battery I'd bought the past spring would last a good four years.

Having a vehicle on the island is a luxury. With most of the year-round population clustered within a ten-minute walk of the ferry, most islanders walk or bicycle. Cars and trucks are sometimes more trouble than they're worth. I don't know anyone who has a garage. After a heavy snow, the snowplow buries cars where they're parked along the shoulder. By the time I shovel out the truck and wait for the windows to defrost I might as well have walked to the boat. And when a vehicle breaks down, it usually sits, or eventually is towed to town on the car ferry for repairs.

There are other noticeable differences on Peaks from mainland communities. For instance, there are no crosswalks. We have no stop signs. Speed limits are not posted. Street signs are largely absent.

What's more, and this *is* a public safety issue when there's an emergency, only a handful of island houses have numbers. It's not uncommon for someone to describe their house location to the police as: *It's the brown two-story cottage with yellow shutters the next left after the Bradbury house, you know, the people with the cat named Oscar.* That night, I hung a left immediately before Brad's bike shop. The woman in labor lived in the fourth house on the left. I pulled over and knocked on the door. After a moment, a slouchy, droopy-eyed, young man wearing painter's overalls cracked open the door.

"Yeah?"

I held up my emergency bag. "Doctor Radis. I'm here to see Liz." He looked at me blankly. A TV blared in the background. In his right hand he held a can of Budweiser. Was that a joint I smelled? "I'm here to see Liz?" I repeated. "She called and thinks she might be in labor."

Inside, two more men lounged on the couch, watching TV, their unlaced boots resting on a coffee table. Magazines and empty beer cans littered the carpet. A stack of wood lay next to a woodstove. I stepped inside. One of the men pointed toward a back room. "Liz! Doctor's here."

"Thanks. Can I use your phone?"

"For what?" The third man on the couch stirred for the first time.

"I need to let the police know that I'm here in case we need to transfer her to town. They can be over in five minutes."

"No police," he said emphatically.

I blinked. The police will need to wait. I'll examine Liz first. It's possible I won't need them. If need be, I can call the Portland Police dispatcher directly in Portland and convince them to send the fireboat without involving the police. The magic words: *woman in labor* is usually enough to start the emergency wheels moving.

Lying on a rumpled bed inside the dimly lit room was Liz. I felt a cool draft on my legs as I removed my parka and draped it over a chair. She laid on her side, facing away from me, her black, stringy, shoulder length hair pulled back over her ears by two silver barrettes. A single, oversized, gold hoop draped off one ear. On the dresser next to the bed was a lighter and several loose cigarettes. Panting and groaning, she was oblivious to my presence.

"Liz? It's me, Dr. Radis, I'm here to check on your labor."

She turned onto her back, the contraction easing, and after a low-pitched groan of relief, licked her lips and swallowed. "It's dry in here."

"And cold, the room is cold," I added.

"Ron said he'd look around for a space heater." Her voice trailed off. "Might as well take a look." In one sweeping movement, she pulled the blanket down to the level of her waist. Pale blue stretch marks flowed off the outer contours of her abdomen. Her arms were pencil thin. A sliver of light angled in from the living room, lighting up her face.

"First baby?" I asked, thinking, *Please let it be a first baby, please let it be a first baby.* First-time labors usually progress S-L-O-W-L-Y.

"Yes. I lost a lot of weight last year, nearly sixty pounds, people said I was getting fat, but I've gained back sixteen with the pregnancy. Dr. Fredericks, at the Maine Med clinic, says I should have gained more, but I don't like being fat. At our last visit a few months ago, she said I was doing fine. The baby was doing fine," she corrected herself.

I opened my emergency kit and pulled on a pair of sterile gloves. Then I squirted a dollop of Vaseline onto the second and third fingers of my left hand. "Liz, I need to do an internal. We need to know how far along you are."

"Sure. I was expecting you'd need to do that." She scooted closer to the edge of the bed. I rested one arm on the closest leg and with the other gently probed the entrance to the vagina. Liz bit down on her lip. "Another contraction is coming."

"Breath through it," I said. "Short, tiny pants. Blow it away. Pick a spot, like the poster on the far wall, and concentrate on it. Don't push. Blow." I probed further up the birth canal with my index and middle finger until I felt the cervix, the entrance to the uterus. It was thinned and partially open, about 3 centimeters. Until she was fully dilated at 10 centimeters, the fetus should remain safely tucked away in the uterus. I exhaled in relief. I had time to call for the fireboat.

"Good news, Liz," I began. "You're in active labor. Your cervix is thinned and partially open. I'm going to call the fireboat. You'll be in town and in the hospital before you know it. Only one thing more, I need to take your blood pressure and listen to the baby's heartrate."

"What time is it?"

"A little after 1:00 am. The last ferry for Portland left hours ago."

"Shit! I thought I could . . . "

I ignored this as I reached over and wrapped a blood pressure cuff around her arm and recorded the blood pressure on a sheet of paper. 156/98. Then I transferred the cuff to the other arm and chewed on my inner lip as I recorded the numbers: No mistake, it was 158/96, nearly the same. The readings wouldn't be of immediate concern if Liz wasn't pregnant. Lifestyle changes, reduced salt, exercise, and smoking cessation would be recommended. But this was different, the numbers were in range for preeclampsia, a serious complication of first pregnancies and often a prelude to eclampsia, a seizure disorder that could occur either during labor or post-delivery. Both Liz and the baby were now in a high-risk category.

Without a word, I placed the stethoscope over my ears and leaned over her abdomen. I couldn't hear the fetal heart sounds. Cracking open the door, I shouted down the hallway, "Please turn down the volume! I'm trying to listen to the baby's heart-rate."

Closing the door, I could hear muffled laughter as one of the men on the couch imitated me in a whiny, pleading voice, but almost immediately the blare of the TV diminished, and I returned to my work. Pressing the stethoscope firmly on the lower abdomen I checked the second hand on my watch as I counted out the heart beats over fifteen seconds and multiplied this by four. A normal fetal heart rate is usually between 120 and 160 per minute, Liz's baby's heart was 120, on the lower end of normal, and reason for concern. With fetal distress, lower rates are often the rule.

Folding away the stethoscope and placing it back inside my green satchel, I said, "Okay, here's where we stand, Liz." I pulled up a chair to the side of the bed. "Here, take a sip of water. You need to keep up your fluids." She leaned forward and eagerly drank from the cup I offered. "Your blood pressure is high and your baby's heartrate is a little low. At the moment, I don't think you or the baby are in immediate danger, but we need to get you to town for the remainder of your labor. You likely have what's called preeclampsia and will need medications we don't have on the island. I'm calling the fireboat."

This was no time to discuss the fine points of my tentative diagnosis. I squeezed her hand and walked back into the hallway. On the wall was the phone. I lifted up the receiver and dialed 911.

"Portland Emergency services, how can I help you?"

"Hi, this is Dr. Radis on Peaks Island. I have a young woman in labor on the island. I'm at the house and she needs to be transferred to Maine Medical Center."

"And are the island police on the scene?"

"No, not yet. I've called their number and they're not answering."

"Then, we need to wait until . . ."

"No, we don't need to wait. The woman is in active labor and has preeclampsia. The baby may be in fetal distress. I need the fireboat underway *now*. The EMTs on the fireboat can call me at this number for more information. Her blood pressure is 156/96. The fetal heart rate is 120. Are you writing this down?"

"Yes."

"We need to move on this." I cradled the phone on my shoulder and opened my emergency converted Sears fishing tackle box on a hallway chair. The compartments unfolded like an accordion, exposing my emergency medications. Good, my medical assistant, Anne, had replaced the 500-cc bag of normal saline I used last week on Cliff Island. I can start an IV before the fireboat arrives.

"What is your address?"

I stretched out the cord line and nudged open the bedroom door with a foot. "Liz, what's your address?"

"We're on Grunder Street."

"Do you know what number?"

"No."

One of the men on the couch grumbled "26." Another said, "No, it's 33, isn't it?"

"I don't know," said a third.

"Operator, I'm on Grunder Street. It's the fourth house on the left coming off Island Avenue. Please notify the police. I'll be looking for them." I hung up the phone and half closed my eyes. Concentrate. The looming issue was that the hypertension of preeclampsia may be a prelude to a seizure. Magnesium sulfate can prevent seizures triggered by preeclampsia, but I didn't have magnesium sulfate in my emergency box. Intravenous Valium is the drug of choice to terminate a seizure. I have that. I tucked the vial into my pocket.

There was a knock on the door. I peeked out the blind. It was Mike and Big John. The three men fled out the back door. Big John ducked his head under the door jam and sniffed as he entered. Mike carried his own emergency box and a canister of oxygen. Mike glanced down at my pants. "Your legs okay? Figured the ripped pants and bloody hands after we jumped off the boat weren't much to worry about. Fireboat's underway; should be here in twenty minutes. Can she walk to the ambulance outside?"

"I think so," I answered. "She's down the hallway. If you can retake her blood pressure while I set up for a heparin lock, I'd appreciate it. Her initial numbers were high." Inside the room, Mike flipped on the light and chatted with Liz as he wrapped the blood pressure cuff around her right arm. I prepped the other arm with an alcohol swab before inserting a large bore needle into a healthy-appearing vein. Then I advanced a catheter over the needle, removed the needle, taped the heparin lock in place and flushed it with a vial of heparin. Okay, we have access if she begins to hemorrhage or seize. Mike flashed me the blood pressure numbers: 162/94.

Outside, the rain changed back to pelting sleet. We bundled Liz up and walked her to the ambulance. Mike drove and I squeezed in next to Liz. Big John, twice too big for the back seat, walked. Mike gently applied the brakes down Welch Street. In the distance, just off House Island, I could see the fireboat.

Liz whimpered as another contraction took hold. She reached up and grabbed Mike's shoulder as I held the IV bag aloft in the front seat. I felt her shiver and suddenly grab a breath and bear down. My rational side noted, first baby, 3 cm dilated, she has a long way to go. My irrational side shrieked, no, no, no, no! Not here, not now! The contraction passed. Liz took several cleansing breaths and relaxed, temporarily. A few minutes later, the fireboat slid into the Public Safety float and two emergency medical technicians (EMTs) hopped off and raced up the ramp. Mike and I wrapped Liz in two blankets and walked her toward the boat. In the lee of the freight shed, I relayed the latest blood pressures to the EMTs and expressed my concern about preeclampsia. As one of them helped Liz board, the other EMT assured me that they were in contact with the Maine Medical Center emergency room. I hesitated at the edge of the ramp, unsure if I should hop on. "Do you have magnesium sulfate or valium?" I asked.

"Yes, on the mag sulfate. Valium? Probably not. We'll get her settled onboard, get a fresh blood pressure, and give them an update in the ER while we're underway. It helps that we have IV access for meds. Thanks. We're good to go."

"Here. Take this," I handed the EMT the vial of IV valium, "Just in case."

Squinting into the wind as the fireboat churned toward Portland, I exhaled deeply and felt my shoulders relax. At the far end of the float, the silhouette of a boat caught my eye. There, neatly tied off on the inside of the public safety float, rocking with the incoming waves, was the *Connolly*.

3

A cool, still, morning mist draped over the channel between Peaks and Great Diamond Island. Frost encased the cattails and rose hips bordering the walkway leading from our house to the street. I paused on the walkway to admire clumps of reed grass and Canada goldenrod, their tasseled, drooping heads now faded with the first cold snap. With a bang and a slam, kindergartener Kate burst through the door of our house and sprinted toward me, sliding to a stop against my knees.

"I'm going to school!" Kate beamed.

"Do you have everything?" I asked.

She patted her lunchbox and backpack and said, "Yes, it's all here!"

"Hat?" I asked. She ran her hand through her knot of yellowed hair, still damp from a morning shower. "Mittens?" She thrust one mitten in my general direction and tried to edge past me. I grabbed a loose arm and pointed her back toward the house. Outside the mudroom door, Sandi stood in her bathrobe, holding Molly in one arm, and the missing hat and mitten in the other.

Kate raced back down the pathway. After snugging the knit cap firmly on our daughter's head, Sandi tied the mittens to a loop extending from the cuff of Kate's jacket. Then she handed her a plastic bag. I reached into my back pocket for my wallet, and finding it empty, hoped that the plastic bag contained not only my wallet, but hopefully, my keys as well. Yes, it did.

Last week at the fall cookout for our island school, Kate's kindergarten teacher had informed Sandi and I that our gangly daughter was a delight but that the class spent considerable time outside walking in the woods and, frankly, with the colder weather, she should be wearing warmer clothes. Sandi and I looked at each other quizzically for a moment before Sandi asked if she could check out the lost and found

21

box inside. It didn't take long to discover that more than half of the box: two coats, a knit cap, numerous gloves, a single shoe? belonged to Kate. Like father, like daughter. Molly, on the other hand, not quite three, folded her PJs and placed them neatly in a drawer. She was Sandi's clone.

Kate scooted ahead, skipping along the edge of our property where a winding, mossy path parallels a seasonal stream as it drops slowly to the beach. I caught her attention and pointed down the path. Atop a rotting red maple stump, a pileated woodpecker hammered into the decaying wood, shards flying in all directions. Suddenly aware of our presence, the bird froze before flapping silently into the lower branches of a nearby red spruce.

Reaching the school yard, Kate dropped my hand and raced over to the monkey bars, where she joined a half-dozen classmates. On the edge of the schoolyard, behind a wire enclosure, plump chickens emerged from their coop. I am reminded of a game Kate said she plays with her friend Tanya. The two capture chickens and fling them as high in the air as humanly possible. The chicken that remains aloft the longest is the winner.

For a few minutes later, the schoolyard was brimming with activity: basketball, kickball, tag. There was some taunting and chasing. The younger children arrived in the company of an adult. The older students traveled in small herds, rode bicycles or skateboarded. Kate often traveled by cartwheel.

There was a rumor that a mother was lobbying the city of Portland to build a sidewalk around the blind curve of Island Avenue a few hundred yards from the school. The idea was ridiculed by some because both before and after the curve there was no plan for a sidewalk. I thought the suggestion was spot on, but many island residents were unconvinced that "Laurie's sidewalk" was necessary. Sidewalk? Next thing you know we'd have curbs and parking meters.

I paused to review the day, as if visualizing our family's near future might lend order out of chaos. It's always worth a try. In a few minutes, Sandi would change into insulated underwear, jeans, and a wool work shirt before dropping Molly off at Angie and John Kelso's day care. She'd work until 2:30 at her part-time job as a plumber/electrician assistant, then pick up Molly before circling back to the grammar school for Kate.

By the end of the day, Sandi would have crawled under several porches to drainpipes, changed a half-dozen diapers, lugged buckets full of tools to job sites, washed several loads of dirty clothes, and rewired an electrical outlet. She was not the only female worker on the crew; her boss, Paul Erico, hired women exclusively. He only thought he ran the show.

For my part, clinic hours started in thirty minutes. I'd see patients until noon, board the twenty-minute ferry to Portland, drive to the hospital, round on my patients, and probably discharge Mrs. Rockefellow who had recovered nicely from a kidney infection. Then I'd reverse course for the 3:15 ferry to Peaks, see patients back at the clinic from 4 to 7 p.m., and hopefully be home before Kate and Molly's bedtime, that is, if I didn't have a house call. To reach my goal, I reminded myself, I'd need to strategically skip a Morbidity and Mortality meeting at the hospital and avoid the doctor's dining room, where I might easily linger over a cup of coffee. On a hunch, I reached into my green satchel and discovered an apple and two Snickers bars. Make that two apples. Thank you, Sandi.

After kissing Kate good-bye, I cut through Snake Alley, one of the island's countless traditional dirt shortcuts connecting neighborhoods through what is technically private property. In summer, garter snakes (exactly how they ended up on Peaks Island is a mystery) are sometimes seen sunning themselves on the rocks lining the alley. By fall, they'll undoubtably be denned up in an underground intertwined ball, ostensibly dead, awaiting resurrection next spring.

Reaching Elizabeth Street, I continued through the corner of an empty overgrown lot and crossed Luther Street, before the path narrowed and emptied out onto Sterling Street. Of course, there are no actual street signs labeling Elizabeth, Luther, or Sterling streets. There *is* a sign with white lettering at the corner of Island Avenue and Sterling Street. It says: *Hospital.* The Island Health Center is not a hospital. It is a simple, cream-colored, two-story cottage with two exam rooms, a handicap ramp on the west side, and flower boxes facing the dirt road. Inside, a simple plaque commemorates the gift of the cottage by Eileen and Ray Herrick in memory of their son Michael.

Sister Mia, arms crossed, cast a skeptical eye in my direction as I briskly strode through the waiting room and greeted Anne, the Island Health Center's receptionist, billing clerk, medical assistant, and only employee. Anne buttoned up her lab coat and adjusted her glasses as she flashed me the morning schedule. "Put on your roller skates this morning, you'll need them." I pick up a stack of charts from my swivel chair and place them on the edge of my desk. There was a wave of sticky notes on lab sheets and x-ray reports. I would transfer names and phone numbers into my 3-by-5 inch At-A-Glance pocket calendar, creating a running to-do-list I'd pick away at between patients.

The converted cottage makes privacy difficult if not impossible (by leaning back in my chair I can see the entire waiting room), but there are advantages to this. For one, I can observe an islander rise from a chair and assess their balance and strength. Are they limping? Anxious? Sullen? Angry? All of this is quietly, perhaps unconsciously filed away. It gives me a subtle edge, a heads up when I enter the exam room.

Take Sister Mia. Dressed in a brown habit and thick supportive hose, she was overlarge for her vinyl chair. The elderly nun had a bob of curled white hair and an oval, open face. Her eyes, gray blue, flickered gentleness one moment and a barking temper the next. Sarge—her nickname from her Catholic school teaching days—had a laundry list of troubles: diabetes, peripheral neuropathy, urinary incontinence, glaucoma, asthma, hyperlipidemia, osteoarthritis, and hypertension, and none of them were well controlled. In my fifth year of caring for Sister Mia, my expectations, but not necessarily my efforts, had become more realistic, more strategic. For instance, my goal for blood pressure control in a hypertensive is ideally, less than 138/84. If this can be pulled off with dietary changes and a single blood pressure medication, I consider this a win.

In Sister Mia's case, we were not winning. I'd changed medications multiple times due to side effects both major and minor. Each time I tried to edge up the dose, there was a call to the health center with the report—pick one: *My mouth is too dry. I'm itching. I can't sleep. I'm too drowsy. I can't think clearly. My mind is racing.* In response, I'd lower the dose or change prescriptions and cross my fingers. No luck. On low-dose captopril, Sister Mia developed a nagging cough. On propranolol, a disturbing wheeze. Clonidine turned her into a *zombie*. Over time we came full circle back to a simple diuretic, a smidgeon of methyldopa, and a program of weight loss and exercise. I'd come to accept that Sister Mia's blood pressure might never fully normalize but rationalized we had both done the best we can.

As I mulled this over, Anne called Sister Mia's name and led her to the scale. The elderly nun was clearly limping. A few minutes later, the two disappeared inside the exam room. I lingered outside the door for a moment, preparing myself for a challenging yet strangely invigorating visit. "Sister Mia, what can I do for you today?"

"Never mind my blood pressure, I know why it's elevated. The pain in my knee; I can barely stand! Sister Janice wants me to join her for a walk, but it's all I can do to drag myself to morning devotions. I'm so frustrated, I went off my diet. But that's not why I'm here; I gave Anne a urine sample. I think I have another bladder infection."

There. In a few brief sentences, I'd been instructed to ignore her blood pressure (circled by Anne in red with an exclamation mark), understood why she was unable to exercise, and prepared myself for uncontrolled blood sugars in the face of an infection.

Where to start? I reached down and palpated the knee. It was clearly swollen. As Sister Anne flexed and extended the joint, it creaked and groaned under my hand. I wrote in the chart: *moderate effusion, medial joint line jump tenderness.* Wait. Wasn't it only a few months ago that Sister Mia had traveled to town for an x-ray of the knee? I flipped through the chart and found the report: *The medial aspect of the left knee demonstrates bone against bone changes consistent with end-stage osteoarthritis.*

I scrunched up my face. I was fully aware that no matter what I did, we couldn't dodge the fact that the knee was completely worn down. She'd need a knee replacement, but. . . I thumbed further into the chart. Shoot, her creatinine, a measure of kidney function, was elevated; her kidneys were functioning at less than 20 percent of normal. I wasn't that surprised; for decades Sister Mia's kidneys had taken the brunt of her hypertension and poorly controlled diabetes. If I asked for a consultation, the orthopedic surgeon's note would undoubtably state: *The patient's renal insufficiency and obesity make her a poor candidate for knee replacement,* code for, *What, are you crazy? No way am I going to operate on this woman.*

I tapped a finger on the table. "Sister Mia, how do you feel about a cortisone injection for the knee?"

"You won't hurt me, will you?" she asked.

I did not want to lie to a nun. "It might hurt a little, but I'll numb it up." With some misgiving, she signed the permit and gripped the armrest like she was ready for takeoff. I cleansed the lateral aspect of the knee, anaesthetized the soft tissues and felt a 'pop' as I entered the joint space with the needle. Sister Mia's grip relaxed and she exhaled. There, the worst was over. Changing syringes with a Kelly clamp, I injected the milky corticosteroid solution, withdrew the needle, and placed a Band-Aid over the puncture site.

"The cortisone should take effect in two or three days. Rosemont pharmacy should send the prescription for your bladder infection on the 4:30 ferry. Jerry can drop it off at the convent. Oh, and take an extra Diabinase, that will increase your total dose to two twice daily. We need better control of your diabetes. I want to see you back a week from today."

The morning flew by. A five-year-old tested positive for strep throat. A man I'd never seen before came in with a painful back and hoped that I could manipulate it. I did, and the procedure seemed to offer him some relief. Dave Quinby arrived with an infection in the palm of his hand where a sea urchin spine punctured his work glove. A husky bear of a man with a ready laugh, he dove year-round for sea urchins, sand dollars, and starfish in the relatively shallow waters of Casco Bay. In a barn adjacent to his house up Sterling Street, Dave and his wife Marcia preserved the daily catch in formaldehyde. The specimens were shipped to Carolina Scientific Products, and from there, to high school and college anatomy classes. It was a unique and sometimes dangerous family business.

Puncture wounds are tricky. By the time I see them, the hole has usually sealed over and only a small, red, tender spot identifies the injection site. But deeper in the soft tissues, a vigorous infection might be spreading. I inspected the palm and pressed on the tissues leading up to the second finger where subtle swelling was present. Dave winced. I started him on an antibiotic and asked him to notify me quickly if the hand didn't improve—occasionally these types of infections require intravenous antibiotics or even the services of a hand surgeon to incise and drain a deep pocket of pus.

Anne led laconic Bobby Emerson into an exam room for a routine EKG. A tall, sinewy man in his 70s with outsized hands and a long loping gait, Bobby was what is known as a "high liner," a lobsterman who year in and year out, out fished his peers. This was in stark contrast to a "dub." Dubs and high liners may place their traps side-by-side, their buoys a mere twenty feet apart, but the result is embarrassingly consistent: empty traps for the dub, lobster-filled traps for the high-liner.

Several winters ago, on the day he nearly died, Bobby passed out twice on his boat pulling lobster traps, but continued to work. Arriving home for lunch, one moment he stood behind his wife, Laura, in their kitchen, the next, he awoke on the floor with Laura on top and a bump on his forehead. His wife convinced him to drive over to the health center, where I was initially reassured that Bobby's heart rate was chugging along at a healthy eighty beats per minute. Then I lightly pressed my stethoscope against his neck to assess for narrowing of the carotid artery. The next thing I knew, Bobby's eyes rolled back, and he passed out but retained a slow regular pulse. When he regained consciousness, I hooked him up to an EKG. The diagnosis was intermittent complete heart block, an indication for a pacemaker. I quickly inserted an IV and called for the fireboat.

When Bobby heard the fireboat was on its way, he said, "Winds blowing, dead low tide," which in the moment seemed to be irrelevant, but in fact summarized our predicament in five simple words. Sure enough, when the fireboat arrived in a raging snowstorm, high winds, and rolling waves rocked it dangerously against the wharf. A rare eleven-and-a-half-foot low tide dropped the fireboat so low below the wharf, that looking back, it's a wonder how we safely belayed Bobby, wrapped in a blanket, lying on a sled, into the waiting arms of the crew on deck.

It was Bobby's emergency that ultimately led to a major upgrade in our emergency transfer system. With state and city funding, a year-round, sturdy public safety float was installed. The float I had jumped onto and nearly rolled off of several nights ago, now rose and fell with the tide and provided a safer platform for emergency transfers.

The second upgrade took time, but was, perhaps, even more critical. The island needed a *real* ambulance. Bobby survived the transfer from the health center to the wharf, but it was in the back of a van, strapped to an orange plastic sled amid rusted tire chains and two shovels.

Although there is a saying, "If you have two islanders, there are three arguments," on the need for an ambulance, island residents spoke with one voice. Islanders wrote letters describing their own harrowing experiences in the back of the rescue van. I attended and testified at a Portland Community Development Grant hearing at city hall. The lobbying paid off. When the ambulance arrived, complete with a modern cushioned bed with collapsible wheels, emergency transfers, though never routine, became less harrowing.

But transfers still remained a daunting, time-consuming, complex process. After all, we lived several miles out to sea. Here's how it works: When an islander with a medical emergency calls 911, the Portland Police dispatcher notifies the police on Peaks. If the police confirm the need for a transfer, a MEDCU team boards the fireboat at the Casco Bay Lines wharf in Portland. Depending on conditions—fog, wind, waves—the trip to Peaks takes fifteen to twenty minutes. By then, the ambulance has usually backed down the wharf, the stretcher wheeled down the ramp, and the patient boards the fireboat. Arriving back in Portland, the gurney is pushed up a ramp to another ambulance. Door to door, from the time an islander calls 911 until they flash through the ER door, takes more than an hour. And that's if everything goes like clockwork.

What about helicopter transfers? In my early years on the island, none of the Portland hospitals was home to a helicopter pad. That's changed, but with Maine's wind and fog, helicopter travel continues to be high risk. Years ago, a helicopter plunged into the bay off the northeast corner of Peaks while carrying a burn victim and his nurse from a community hospital up the coast to Maine Medical Center. Only the pilot survived. In my mind, the dependability of the fireboat far outweighs any potential time advantage of helicopter transfer.

This morning, Bobby's EKG confirmed that his pacemaker is functioning as a failsafe safety net. I asked him about the lobster season. "Caught a few. Done for the year. I'm pulling my boat this weekend if the weather holds. Ricky Crowley said he'd lend a hand. Want to help?" For Bobby, this was a veritable speech. I readily agreed, schedule permitting.

I glanced at the clock as I scribbled a note. Twenty minutes before the ferry. At my desk I eyed a stack of incomplete charts. The door squeaked open; it was Lois Herndon, one of my favorite islanders.

But today, she could hardly walk. Anne grabbed Lois's elbow and ushered her into an exam room. A moment later, Anne emerged holding several red-top and blue-top test tubes filled with blood. "Lois hurts all over," she reported. "I hope you don't mind; I figured you might need some blood. I'll spin the red-top tube down and fill out the paperwork for the hospital lab. You can decide on the way to town what lab you want to order."

"Knock on the door with eight minutes to go," I answered. "I need to round on my patients at the hospital and can't miss the afternoon ferry." Then I pushed open the door and greeted Lois as if I had all the time in the world.

"Dr. Radis," Lois lifted her head, her face drawn and pinched. "Thank you so much for fitting me in. I know you have a ferry to catch, but to be truthful, I couldn't even get out of bed this morning. I'm moving slightly better now, but I still feel absolutely pathetic."

"I understand. When you're sick, the last place you want to drag yourself to is a doctor's office. Cough?

"No."

"Sore throat?"

"No."

"Abdominal pain? Diarrhea?"

"No."

Lois groaned as she shifted on the exam table. "I feel stiff and weak, like I suddenly became an old woman with a bad case of embalming."

I reviewed the possibilities. It was too early in the season for influenza. Another viral syndrome? Parvovirus perhaps? That would be unusual in an adult, but I tucked it away in my differential diagnosis. A medication side-effect? No, Lois was on no prescription meds. I lifted up Lois's pants leg and checked her chest and abdomen for signs of the tell-tale erythema chronicum rash of Lyme disease. Nothing.

I continued my questioning as I assessed her muscle strength and palpated the hands and elbows and knees for signs of inflammation. Except for excruciating pain moving her shoulders and hips, her exam was normal.

"Are you weak?"

"No."

"Painful eyes?"

"No."

"Headache? Stiff neck?"

"No, not really."

I laid her down and listened to her heart and lungs and palpated her abdomen. Normal.

I didn't know what was wrong.

Anne knocked on the door. "I have your bag packed. Don't forget to drop off the laboratory specimens at the hospital. Sister Mia's urine culture is double-wrapped."

Lois could barely sit up. The process looked extraordinarily uncomfortable. I laid a hand on her shoulder. "I'm going to run some tests on your blood. We'll look for signs of infection and inflammation. In the meantime, I want you to take these samples of indomethacin, an anti-inflammatory, it may help some with your muscle and joint stiffness." I unlocked a drawer and packaged a dozen of the capsules into a simple brown envelope. "One with each meal. They can irritate your stomach so remember, take them with food."

"Go!" Lois swept her hand in the air. "I have every confidence you'll figure this old broad's problem out. To the ferry boat!"

As I hustled past the check-out counter, Anne looked at her watch. "Take my bicycle. You have four minutes."

I straddled the rusted one-speed, and rose up on the pedals to gain speed. It was going to be close. Between Plante's Marina and the Cock-eyed Gull restaurant, I caught a glimpse of the *Machigonne* where a deckhand was helping a young mother with a toddler pull her cart over the lip of the gangplank. She disappeared into the hold. Hanging a right onto Welch Street, the hill of mechanical mishaps, I waved to Lisa puffing on a cigarette outside her coffee shop and swooshed past her, skidded to a halt at the end of the wharf, and jogged across the gangplank.

As the ferry pulled away, I gazed back at the wharf. Did I lock Anne's bike? I squinted in the direction of the newspaper stand and, then pulled out my pocket calendar and wrote: *Tonight! coming off ferry, remember Anne's bike!*

4

I was alone on the upper deck of the ferry, in the lee of the smoke-
stack, as a brisk raw wind kicked up whitecaps off Fort Gorges. On
the 6:15 morning ferry from Peaks, this spot would normally be a
gathering place for a small group of irreverent, witty, and bitingly sar-
castic men who disdained the crowded hold. No one asks me questions
about their health or wonders what I think about the newest medical
advances. I'm not even sure if everyone knows that I'm a doctor; none
of them see me as patients. As much as I enjoy the company of my boat
friends, I realize how little time I spend nurturing those friendships on
dry land.

I took a deep breath and exhaled, feeling my shoulders relax, aware
that my life was unbalanced. It was full. It was rewarding, but I never
seemed to stop walking, bicycling, boating, or driving to my next
patient encounter. A life in medicine is by its very nature, unbalanced.
The long hours studying in medical school followed by the grind of
a residency prepared me for the responsibilities of patient care, but it
came with significant cost. Over time, doctors often feel isolated, over-
stressed, and, particularly when we inevitably lose a patient or imple-
ment the wrong treatment plan, at risk of burning out. Even in the
five short years I'd been in practice, I'd seen colleagues who began, as I
had, drinking a late evening beer to relax before bedtime. Over time,
the beer becomes two or three. The occasional sleeping pill (which I'd
avoided), becomes a habit. Over time, it all too frequently unravels.

The strain of my Peaks Island and Chebeague Island clinics, caring
for hospitalized patients, office hours in my Portland office, not to mention an occasional house call to the outer islands, was taking a toll. It
wasn't unusual for me to leave home before the children were awake and
to return long after their bedtime. Sandi, sometimes for weeks at a time,
was more like a single parent than a partner in an equitable marriage.

The strain in our marriage reached a point the past year that we went to counseling. That helped. I made some changes in my schedule; eventually reducing my Chebeague Island clinic from two days to one and resigned from several hospital committees. Sandi made some adjustments of her own. The evening meal on the dairy farm she grew up on was a time when the family sat down together and shared the events of the day. Supper brought everyone together and up to date. It's been difficult for her to let go of the expectation that I can regularly sit down for an evening meal. When she quit her job as a family therapist in Portland and began part-time plumbing and electrical work on the island, her work-family balance dramatically improved overnight.

My dad was the son of Italian immigrants and, like many immigrants, his nose was in a book as soon as he could hold one. He became a chemical engineer and eventually designed and operated plants for the Monsanto Chemical Corporation. My mother Shirley grew up on a farm in West Virginia without indoor plumbing during the depression. Despite formidable obstacles, she became a nurse. When I was 11, in the summer of 1964, the year the surgeon general declared cigarettes to be a risk factor for heart disease, my father arrived home and suffered a massive, fatal heart attack. He was 43. After my dad died, my two brothers and I, each in our uniquely damaged way, coped as best we could. Only now, as an adult with my own spouse and children, did I realize the depth of my mother's loss. She never remarried.

Growing up, I had good friends; that probably saved me.

Through high school and college, I made a conscious effort to avoid my father's fate; I never picked up his cigarette habit, and though interested in chemistry, gravitated toward the soft sciences, initially dreaming of a career as a paleontologist before switching gears to marine biology—anything to keep me outdoors. And I kept a saying in mind for whenever I felt I was devoting too much time to studies and not enough to fun: *Always leave yourself an out.*

I skated through my first two years of college. It would not be inaccurate to say that I majored in pool, particularly eight ball, but a chance meeting with a bush pilot doctor in Baja, Mexico, on a long bicycle ride changed my trajectory. The doctor was an osteopathic physician, a DO, and I was intrigued by his holistic, empathetic approach to patient care.

I decided to become a doctor, an osteopathic physician. It took time to undo the damage to my early academic record, but scoring well on the MCAT, the standardized test for medical school, didn't hurt.

Now I was grinding out the same hours my father did. I worried about that. Fortunately, at the end of the day, Sandi wanted to hear about my frustrations and small successes, and I, in turn, was fascinated by her connection to real work. By that, I mean finishing a job with tangible results: a sink that no longer leaked, a toilet that flushed cleanly, a light switch that flipped on and off. It was remarkable that she'd made the transition from social work to plumbing, but as she said, "The difference isn't as much as you might think. At the end of the day, one way or the other, you're still dealing with people's sh—t."

I enjoyed the challenge of managing with limited resources in an island practice, making the correct diagnosis relying on a focused history and physical exam and basic lab. X-rays and specialist consultations in Portland are critically necessary for some patients but learning who needs what and when was an intriguing and challenging aspect of island practice. If I was going to convince sick patients to travel to the mainland, I needed to constantly ask myself the question: *Would the results of the test, change treatment?*

For instance, if a patient had a productive cough with green sputum and a fever and I auscultate crackles in the left lung, did I need a chest x-ray to confirm the diagnosis of pneumonia? No. On the other hand, if there were red flags in their history: heavy smoking, weight loss, blood in the sputum, it was absolutely necessary to obtain a chest x-ray to ensure that lung cancer wasn't lurking in the background.

Twenty minutes later, the ferry throttled down as we passed the Maine State Pier and angled into the Casco Bay Lines wharf. A line of double-crested cormorants skimmed the water heading south. Two immature loons, a black and white male bufflehead, and a flock of skittish long-tailed ducks parted for the ferry to pass. A seal popped up, scavenging fish entrails from a bait business on the adjacent wharf. It was much larger than our usual harbor seals, and I wrote an entry in my pocket planner to look up what in god's name was the ugly seal with the horse-head profile.

Arriving at the Osteopathic Hospital of Maine (OHM) where I was on staff, I made a beeline for the second floor, where I suspected Peaks Islander, Mrs. Rockefellow, age 76, frail and underweight, impatiently awaited discharge. But what exactly is an osteopathic hospital? And how did it come to pass that MDs and DOs (Doctors of Osteopathic Medicine), practice in separate hospitals?

This schism between MDs and DOs goes back to the 1870s when the founder of osteopathic medicine, A.T. Still, developed a holistic approach to the complex connections between mind and body. Flowing from this was his development of osteopathic manipulative therapy (prior to the development of chiropractic therapy) as an adjunct to traditional medical management. Four-year osteopathic medical schools were founded. DOs were often denied staff privileges in MD institutions, so they founded their own hospitals, where they delivered babies, operated on hot appendices, and managed infections. Residencies in family practice, surgery, internal medicine, pediatrics, and a host of other specialties were established.

For decades, a divide remained: MD hospitals didn't accept DO training, and in turn, DO hospitals did not accept MD training. In my early years of practice, between 1985 and 1991, before hospitals opened up their staffs to both DOs and MDs, the two professions, while in many ways similar in their approach to illness, remained entirely separate.

At osteopathic medical schools, in addition to traditional courses in anatomy, physical diagnosis, immunology, and physiology, students take classes in osteopathic principles and practice and learn manipulative skills. At my own hospital, OHM, there is an active department of manipulative medicine. These physicians' skills are utilized in the management of patients with pain limiting their post-op recovery or as an adjunct to treatment of pneumonia or asthma, not solely for more traditional indications in patients admitted with musculoskeletal disorders.

This transition was already underway during the early 1980s when I graduated from the Kansas City College of Osteopathic Medicine. Today, most patients don't even notice if their doctor's lapel indicates whether they are an MD or a DO. Occasionally though, when I least expect it, the old prejudices rear their head, and a patient will be noticeably uncomfortable with my DO degree. In fact, it happened recently. A middle-aged woman, new to the island, made an appointment at the health center for management of her diabetes. She made it all the way into the exam room before she noticed my degree on the wall above the sink. Gathering her purse and coat, she informed Anne on the way out, "I had no idea that Dr. Radis was an osteopath."

Mrs. Rockefellow was anxious to be discharged when I entered her room. Yesterday was the first day she was afebrile during her four-day hospital admission for pyelonephritis, an infection in her right kidney. Not surprisingly, she was dressed to the nines and raring to go. That is, dressed to the nines in hospital slippers, wearing a pearl necklace and a bright floral sundress under a hospital gown. She was still attached to her IV. She swayed sideways as she stood to greet me. "Dr. Radis, I don't know *when* I've felt this good. My nurse says she only needs your okay to pull my IV and spring me loose!' I sat down on the edge of her bed and reviewed the chart. There is an old saying that internists are like fleas, the first to jump on a dog and the last to jump off. We strive to be thorough. We like data. We don't like to be rushed.

"You've met my husband, Perry before, haven't you?" Mrs. Rockefellow pointed over my shoulder. Unbeknownst to me, her husband, Perry, deafer than a cod, was anxious to get their car in line for the next ferry. I raised my hand for him to hold his question and returned to the chart. Okay, white blood count trending downward, repeat urine cultures no growth, ultrasound of the kidney—no abscess or obstruction, kidney function stable, hmm . . . the final report on the bacteria on her urine culture indicated that it was more resistant than first reported. The only oral option was ciprofloxin, a newly approved antibiotic by the Food and Drug Administration. I picked up the phone and called Rosemont pharmacy to see if they had it in stock. They did, and promised me it would be on the 4:30 ferry to Peaks Island. I raised an eyebrow at the cost.

"You're set to go Mrs. Rockefellow. I called in your antibiotic. It should be down on the late afternoon ferry."

"Is it expensive?" Mr. Rockefellow shouted.

"Yes. Your wife has a severe infection and the usual antibiotics won't cure it," I shouted back.

"We have an antibiotic at home. I know where it is; it's in the refrigerator. We'll be fine."

"No, she needs this new antibiotic, it's called ciprofloxin."

"Hippo boxing? What kind of a name is that? Is it expensive?"

I turned to Mrs. Rockefellow and quietly explained the situation. She graciously took my hand and whispered, "I pay the bills. We'll be fine."

The family practice resident wrote a discharge note and I co-signed it. On a typical day, she rounded on fifteen patients with three different attendings, admitted patients from the emergency room, and tracked down lab and x-ray results. Depending on the service, she may be required to start IVs, insert subclavian lines, and pass Foley catheters and nasogastric tubes. If she was the first physician to respond to a code, she might initiate CPR, insert an endotracheal tube, or defibrillate a patient.

My cohort of Peaks Island patients (with an occasional Chebeague admission) were fewer in number than the other attendings she rounded with but were what I would describe as high need. Like Mrs. Rockefellow, they might angle for early discharge. If they required outpatient physical therapy, community health nursing, or counseling, this complicated their discharge and needed to be set up with the ferry schedule in mind.

As I continued my rounds with the family practice resident physician on my remaining four patients, I peeked at my watch. To make the 3:15 ferry back to Peaks, I'd need to be out the door by 2:50. No problem.

As I eased out of the parking lot, I felt relaxed and in control. It was a mirage. Abruptly, I remembered Lois Herndon's blood work and Sister Mia's urine culture. Shoot! I pulled a U-turn, parked, jogged to the first-floor lab, dropped off the specimens and paperwork, and flew out of the parking lot. I was not going to look at my watch. I should be fine. Fifteen minutes later, I pulled into the Widgery Wharf parking lot and couldn't help myself. 3:08. It was going to be close.

Jogging down Commercial Street, I hung a right onto the Casco Bay wharf, and accelerated. Up ahead, the *Machigonne's* gangplank slid onboard. Two crewmen loosened the lines. I waved my green satchel in the direction of the pilot house. Captain Tracy glanced my way and sphinxlike, gazed out into the inner harbor. I came to a stop at the edge of the landing, chest heaving, hands on my knees . . . and the gangplank . . . clanged back onto the wharf. Yes!

Thank you, Captain Tracy.

Settling onto a green bench, I took out my pocket planner and scribbled: *Buy boat.*

5

Although Chebeague Island is only six miles from Peaks by water, reaching it is no easy task. From Peaks, you can't reach Chebeague by ferry. Our dedicated ferry runs back and forth from Peaks to Portland. That's why I was driving thirty minutes up the coast to board the *Islander*, a small ferry operated by the Chebeague Transportation Company.

I daydream about how I can cut my commuting time. A number of water taxi services have come and gone over the years but there isn't enough business beyond the summer months to make a go of it. The police boat? Between blown engines and incompetent captains, I'd be better off swimming. My own boat? When my first boat, a center-console Sea-Whaler, sank on its mooring two years ago, I'd swore off boats. But that was then. If I had a boat, there's no question I'd have more time with Sandi and the children. And there's a classic Maine saying, "You haven't learned much until you've sunk your first boat."

Boarding the *Islander*, I sat facing the stern, nearly hypnotized by the glassy, expanding wake as it rocked several lobster boats in the quiet channel. A seal popped up with the same unfamiliar silhouette I'd seen yesterday. This time I was sure; the guide book I consulted last night before bed captured it perfectly: *Gray seal: halichoerus gryus: hook-nosed sea pig, or horse-head. The male is plain and simply an ugly seal.*

Although undoubtedly, I'd seen gray seals before, at a quick glance, every seal registered in my mind's eye as a harbor seal. It was not the only time I'd lumped similar species together: common double-crested cormorant and its slightly larger cousin, the black cormorant; common goldeneye and Barrow's goldeneye; a simple common crow and a raven. Similar, but entirely different species.

I wondered how many rare disorders I'd missed? What rare diseases, similar in some respects to more common illnesses had passed me by?

Or, as the eminent physician Ron Anderson, from the Brigham and Women's Hospital in Boston, once said, "That disease saw me a long time before I saw it."

Arriving at the Stone Harbor wharf, I bought a cup of coffee and a bag of salted vinegar potato chips at the store and located the key under the floor mat of the Ford pick-up on loan for my weekly clinic. I rolled down the window in the sun-warmed cab and slowly exhaled. I was looking forward to seeing my patients.

Chebeague is twice again as large as Peaks, with less than half as many year-round residents. The main road flows through gently rolling wood lots and open meadows through the interior. Glimpses of Casco Bay, for the most part, are seen at the end of private drives or on the wharves and boat yards scattered here and there on the waterfront. Work centers around lobstering, boat building, and carpentry.

I pulled into the public safety lot and Albion Miller emerged from his ancient Buick. Emerged is a generous description, more like unspooled. Now in his mid-80s, Albion's spindly legs bowed at the knee, giving him a rolling, wobbly gait. He was clean shaven, stooped, and atrophied. Pencil-thin arms dangled from his shoulders from rotator cuff tears in both shoulders. In his prime, he'd fished for cod—when there was still an inshore cod fishery off Chebeague—in a hand-made double-ended dory, setting nets by hand. Like many former fishermen, he knitted, passing away the winter months fashioning scarves and sweaters and mittens.

In the four years I had followed Albion, I had removed cancerous lesions on his face, maintained his blood pressure within a reasonable range, referred him to a urologist for management of an enlarged prostate, and injected a trigger finger on his hand. When the snow flies, I wear the rainbow-colored, double-ribbed scarf he knit for me. He is my biggest supporter on Chebeague.

Chebeague is an island of contrasts. Wealthy summer people have made Chebeague their second home for generations. These families proudly identify themselves as "Chebeague Islanders," and are often deeply involved with the community, joining island organizations and donating to various island projects. Then there are the lobstering families and boat builders, and those who tend to the island's infrastructure—carpenters, plumbers, and landscape workers, who generally live inland, off the water, and may lack health insurance. As compared to say, Martha's Vineyard, the second group far outnumbers the first, and traditional, year-round voices, at least by my observation, still have the upper hand in island politics.

I unlocked the exam room and Albion hobbled in. My "office" was a single room with a Civil War era exam table, a corner desk and two chairs. Beneath the exam table was a drawer for patient gowns. On the wall hung a black rotary telephone and a framed oil painting of a fishing boat on loan by a local artist. A slant of light beamed down amid the approaching storm onto the deck as the solitary fisherman pointed the dory toward safe harbor.

On Chebeague my onsite diagnostic tools—in addition to my stethoscope, otoscope, and ophthalmoscope—were limited to a glucometer, urinary dipsticks for urinalysis, a handful of assays to assess for blood in the stool, strep throat, and mononucleosis, and a hand-held ultraviolet Wood's lamp to diagnose fungal skin infections. In the cupboard was a suturing and wound tray along with samples of antibiotics. I made frequent use of a centrifuge to spin down blood samples for the hospital laboratory.

As I stocked the shelves with supplies from town, Albion settled into his chair and whistled a mournful tune. He said the song came to him one day while out on the bay pulling his nets. "A man could make a living close to shore in those days. Cod, haddock, black flounder, herring, scallops, lobster; take your pick depending on the season."

"So, what can I do for you today, Albion?" I asked formally, opening his chart and clicking my pen.

Albion's face drooped. "I thought we might talk about a pill for the winter," he whispered. Albion tap-tapped his fingernail on the edge of the chair and grimaced slightly as he readjusted himself on the wooden seat. "Well now, that's why I'm here, isn't it?" He seemed to be addressing himself. "The full out is that winter and I don't get along eye to eye. For another month, I can still get out to the Stone Wharf for coffee with the boys, but soon enough the weather will turn; that means more time alone, inside. That's when my mind goes dark and it's all I can do to get up in the morning. Thing is, come spring, it usually passes. The sun perks me up."

I reached over and patted Albion lightly on the arm. Since my next patient wasn't due for another twenty minutes, I leaned back in my chair and asked him about his life on Chebeague. Like any man his age, he'd experienced his share of losses, some tragic. I also probed whether he was ever depressed enough to consider taking his own life. "No," he answered. "I've never been that low. For all these years, I've always known that it's temporary, soon as the sun rises higher in the sky, I can feel my mood shift. Course now, I'm fit as a fiddle." He arose and did a semblance of a jig, intent on lightening the mood.

"You know, Albion," I think we can come up with a plan, and part of that would be a low dose of an anti-depressant. We'll start now, before your mood drops; these medications often take time to have an effect. Then we can adjust the dose, depending on whether the initial dose is effective."

Albion slapped his thigh, "By Jiminy, I knew you'd have a plan. You say there's something else we might try?"

"That's right. You have what's called seasonal affective disorder. Depression is common here in Maine as the days grow shorter. What do you think about purchasing a special light you can sit under each morning for a few hours? It emits what's called full-spectrum light, and there's some evidence it can help with your type of depression."

Albion gathered his belongings and took out his wallet. "A light you say? I'm all for that. Now, how much I owe you for the visit? I'm not one for building up a debt."

I squirmed in my seat. Asking for my fee continues to be a difficult task. "I have to submit your bill to Medicare, Albion. I'm not permitted to take your money up front for the visit." Amid his sincere protestations, I ushered him out the door and assured him that Medicare would take care of eighty percent of the fee and I could collect the remainder at a future visit. The problem with this approach is that I could lose track of the twenty percent co-pay. I was sure there was some type of billing reminder I could develop so I could stay on top of that.

I scribbled a note on Albion as my pager went off. It was the internal medicine resident at the hospital. "When will you be by this afternoon? We have a new admission."

"I'm looking at around 2:30. I've got a few more patients here to see and then a house-call. If I miss the scheduled ferry, I believe I can get one of the lobstermen to take me across to the mainland."

"Lobster boat? That's cool. Oh, one more thing, lab called me with results on one of your patients. They're sending a copy to the Peaks Island Health Center. It's on . . . let me see, it's a sedimentation rate on Lois Herndon. The sed rate is 116. That's off the chart, isn't it?"

"Yes, anything over 100 indicates intense inflammation." Hanging up, I turned over the details of Lois's case in my mind: Of course, it *would be* a family friend with an unknown illness. Until a week ago, she was entirely well, then came the aching muscles, morning stiffness, and malaise. What *was* going on with her?

I opened the door for my next patient. The not unpleasant aroma of saltwater, seaweed, and tidal mud flats, with a splash of deodorant flowed into the room. Ben Shipman extended a hand. "Dr. Radis, nice to finally meet you. Take it easy on that grip, I got something brewing in my hands." It was definitely the lobsterman I watched baiting traps on my way to Chebeague several hours ago. "And this is my wife, Laurie." The young couple sat in folding chairs next to the exam table. Ben pointed at the wall. "Hey, Laurie, that's the old painting of Albion Miller on his boat trying to outrun a storm off Outer Green Island." Taking a closer look for the first time at the details of the painting, I could see the same man who'd left my office only minutes before, but a good forty years younger.

"He's lucky he didn't drown more than once," Laurie said. "Sooner or later, it catches up with you."

"Ben, what can I do for you today?"

In response, the lobsterman held up his swollen fingers and lifted up his workpants. The knees were swollen. Both ankles were swollen. Both elbows were swollen. "When I get up in the morning," Ben said, "it's all I can do to lug my sorry butt to the bathroom. Luckily, after I take a good long shower, I start to limber up. By the time I get down to the dock, I can manage the wheel on the *Laurie Anne*, but my power's gone. Funny thing, as long as I keep moving, the pain's not so bad."

"How long ago did it start?" I asked.

"Two, maybe three months ago."

"How can you say that Ben?" Laurie looked up from her notes, "You were complaining of the stiffness in your hands and feet when you prepped the boat for lobstering last spring."

"Well . . . maybe she's right there. At first, I thought that maybe a pebble or tack was stuck in my shoes; my toes ached something terrible, but it's been spreading like some zombie spell."

"Doctor Radis," Laurie cut in. "Ben's crying in his sleep. He doesn't know, but I hear him moaning and groaning."

I winced internally; this was about as bad as it gets. From the look of his joints, Ben Shipman was one step away from being completely disabled. On the posterior aspect of his right elbow was a discrete nodule. It was definitely a rheumatoid nodule. Even without laboratory studies, the diagnosis was clear. There was no reset button for his disease, no ten-day course of a medication to put it to sleep. Rheumatoid arthritis had taken hold of him, and, like a junkyard dog, the disease refused to release him from its grasp.

Finishing my exam, I decided to be straightforward and definitive. "Ben, unfortunately, we're dealing with rheumatoid arthritis." I let this settle in for a moment, and continued. "It's in the family of autoimmune diseases; your own immune system is attracted to the lining of your joints where it's setting off swelling and inflammation. It's overreacting to proteins that are a normal part of you but, perhaps, have been subtly altered. Anyone else in the extended family have RA?"

Momentarily, Ben and Laurie were silent. Then Ben straightened up and said, "My uncle and one of his kids have rheumatoid arthritis. They're shells of their past selves."

"Well, that's not going to be your future," I said. "We have three goals in the treatment of RA; reduce pain, maintain function, and sometimes the most difficult of all, prevent future damage. We'll start with a long-acting anti-inflammatory, it's called piroxicam. It's only one pill a day. If you take it with your evening meal, it should help reduce the severe stiffness and swelling in the morning."

"Is it expensive?"

"No, it's been around for a while, so there's a generic."

"Sounds like a plan." With effort, Ben stood to leave. "Got to get back to work."

"One more thing," I said. "I'd like to refer you to a rheumatology specialist in Portland. I want their opinion on what disease modifying medication we should begin. Piroxicam can help with the pain and stiffness, but it doesn't prevent damage."

"Any chance they can give you advice over the phone and I can follow-up here? Catching two ferries, and driving to Portland, is more or less an all-day trip."

I considered this. "No. I think they'll need to examine you to develop a treatment plan. After the initial visit, I can follow you here on Chebeague to make sure you're not having side-effects from the medications and adjust the dose. Roll up your sleeve, I need to draw a few tubes of blood. The rheumatologist will want the results before they see you."

Ben gathered himself and after a second try brought himself to a standing position. I watched him hobble to the door and called him back. "Ben, one more thing, to jump start this, I can drain the knees and inject them with cortisone. It's not a permanent fix, but it will help until the rheumatologist can get a disease modifying drug onboard."

Ben lay down on the table and I aspirated a cup full of fluid from each knee before injecting depo-Medrol, a form of corticosteroid. The removal of the fluid immediately had a salutary effect on the knees; when Ben stood, they felt looser, more like his old knees. A broad smile spread across his face. "Hey! Good deal!" Laurie, hand me that bottled water from your purse." She handed Ben the unopened bottle and he twisted the top off, or rather, attempted to twist the top off. His fingers refused to flex with enough power to twist off the cap. Suddenly, he flung the bottle against the far wall in frustration. For a moment, we sat in stunned silence.

Ben's shoulders sagged and he briefly bowed his head. "Sorry. These last few months have been tough. Thanks for seeing me today." Then he reached into his back pocket and pulled out a ball cap, snugged it on his head, and walked out to his truck.

In my day planner, I wrote: *Arrange for rheumatology consult. Review treatment of rheumatoid arthritis.*

That night, for the first time in weeks, I caught an early ferry home. At the end of our leisurely dinner, Sandi said, "I forgot to mention. I spoke with Lois Herndon earlier this afternoon. She's such a lovely person."

"What's it been, three years since we adopted her cat, Isabel?" I said, spooning up a last mouthful of ice-cream.

"Yes, and Isabel reminds me of Lois, elegant, genteel, and funny. Anyway, Lois would like you to give her a call tonight. She said you'd know what it's about."

I rubbed the back of my neck and glanced at the clock. It shouldn't wait till tomorrow. I pushed away from the table and dialed Lois's number. After eight rings I hung up. "No answer. That's odd," I said to Sandi. "Okay if I bring Kate with me over to Lois's house?"

"That's fine. Try to be home in less than an hour for Molly's bedtime."

"I can do that," I answered. Kate was already in high-energy mode from the ice cream, but the idea of taking a ride in the truck after dinner was a second dessert. Five minutes later we pulled up in front of Lois's cottage. I knocked on the door and it edged open. Poking my head inside, I yelled, "Lois! Are you there?"

From her bedroom down the hallway, I heard a muffled, "Yes! I'm as here as possible, which isn't saying much."

I put a finger to my lip and instructed Kate, "Remember Lois? She's Isabel's mommy. She doesn't feel well, so use your indoor voice."

Holding onto Kate's hand, we passed a phone on the kitchen wall and entered Lois's dimly lit bedroom. "Oh, isn't this marvelous," Lois brightened, "you've brought Kate! My dear Kate, you must tell me what Isabel is up to. You do know that Isabel lived here with me before she decided to be your cat?"

Kate stuck her thumb in her mouth, a habit she fell back on when she was anxious. On the bookshelf above Lois's bed I noticed a coffee-table volume, *Cats of the World*. "Lois, do you mind if Kate looks at your cat book while we visit?"

"Oh, what a splendid idea. Kate, if you go to page ten, there's a cat on a pillow the spitting image of Isabel. They must be sisters. Speaking of sisters, what are you and Molly wearing for Halloween?"

I opened the book and set it on the carpet. "Kate has a princess outfit and Molly, well, we're not sure." Kate sat against the far wall and balanced the book on her lap as she eagerly turned the pages. "Now Lois, what is it you want to talk with me about? Are you on the mend?"

"Well, actually, no. The muscles, if anything, are getting worse and now I have this awful headache above my eye."

"I'm so sorry." I reached over and palpated her forehead. Lois grimaced. The temporal artery beneath my fingertip felt ropey, the pulse diminished. Suddenly, it made perfect sense; the muscle stiffness, the elevated sedimentation rate, the headaches; Lois was suffering from a disorder I'd read about but never seen: giant cell arteritis. I focused on what little I could recall about the condition. Temporal arteritis is a disorder of the elderly. Incapacitating muscle stiffness is often present in the shoulder and hip girdle. Headaches in the temporal region occur in nearly all patients. The diagnosis is made by surgical biopsy of the affected temporal artery. Something else, there was something else. I ran a free hand through a shock of thinning, sandy hair, thinking. There was something else.

"Oh, and you might find this of interest," Lois continued. "I dragged myself to the bathroom several hours ago, and that was an adventure. It felt like someone dug me up from a fresh grave. Then a gray veil descended over my right eye. I know it was my right eye because I covered the eye with my hand and I could see perfectly well out of the left. In a minute or two, it passed."

Of course! Blindness. The episode Lois experienced was almost certainly amaurosis fugax, a warning that permanent blindness was imminent. "Lois, I need to leave you for a few minutes. I'm going to open up the health center and bring back a medication you should start tonight."

"And that medicine is?"

"Prednisone. You need a big dose of prednisone."

"Oh my. I know about prednisone. It's the fat medicine. You turn into a blimp on prednisone."

"Yes, prednisone has long-term side-effects, but there's no other choice, it's the only medication available to control the disease. That gray veil you experienced coming down over your eye was a warning; the next time it occurs you could lose vision permanently." Lois looked deflated. My explanation felt detached and unfeeling. Here Lois was one of my closest friends on the island and I was holding forth as if I were reading from a textbook. In that moment I realized it was time for a different tack. "We'll aim for less than a five-hundred-pound weight gain, certainly no more than four-hundred," I said with a straight face. "I'll unlock the health center and return in a few minutes with your first dose of prednisone. "I hope your bed is reinforced, it's not unusual to gain more than a hundred pounds with the initial dose." A lop-sided grin spread across Lois's face. "You are pathetic," she whispered. "I'll take the prednisone."

"Daddy, I saw you wink." It was Kate, leaning against the bed with her head on the edge of Lois's pillow. "That was a joke. I saw you do it."

6

I harvested three good-size pumpkins from my garden, and that night their candle-lit grins cast elongated shadows up the front walkway. Halloween on Peaks has a decidedly old-fashioned vibe. The stage at the Lion's Club meeting hall is transformed into a ghoulish fun house. Feeney's Market and the Legion Hall give out candy. Lisa's coffee shop gives out candy. The candy shop gives out candy.

Trees and shrubs on the side-streets off Island Avenue are draped in cobwebs and dangling skeletons. A plastic bat on a wire slides from the top of a front door to the mailbox. Bobby Emerson's mounted deer head screeches at approaching children. Say this about Bobby, if he isn't lobstering, he's thinking about deer or thinking about hunting deer. The man loves his venison.

The celebration is so popular that the 4:30 and 5:35 ferries from town deliver boatloads of children and their parents from Portland, adding to the chaos. My mother Shirley and her sister Izzy time their yearly visit from West Virginia to Peaks Island specifically for Halloween. After arriving on the car ferry yesterday in Izzy's Chevy Impala, their plan was to park in front of the post office and trail behind us, observing the fun at a discreet distance, allowing us precious family time.

Kate was dressed as a princess; Molly was a dog; Sandi and I sported matching battery-powered glowing wool caps. Families with young children, some pushing carriages, traveled from house to house in small groups. As darkness descended, the back streets filled with teenagers hauling pillowcases full of loot. Kate skittered ahead with a friend. A brisk, raw wind flowed off the water. Molly started to shiver and we picked up our two-year-old dog-child and wrapped her in a blanket. Kate circled back. She seemed tentative, and I worried that the entire scene was a bit overwhelming. She leaned against Sandi's legs and announced, "I'm a little bit scared and a little bit happy."

Neighbors Karen and Phil joined us briefly with their son, Charley, who was dressed as a vampire. Phil pulled a wagon with a ragged, candle-lit pumpkin onboard and explained that only thirty minutes ago, he'd dropped by a friend's house and left the pumpkin and wagon briefly on the edge of the street. When he looked back, a buck nonchalantly raised its head from the glowing pumpkin, its face bearded by stringy, orange pulp. The candle was still lit.

Molly fell asleep. We took turns cradling her in our arms. Kate, newly energized by a chocolate bar, ran off with her friend, Nicole. The two scampered up the steps to Lois Herndon's cottage and Lois, decked out in a flowing white gown, opened the door. It had been a week since the biopsy confirmed the diagnosis of temporal arteritis. She moved freely and gracefully; the prednisone I prescribed had done its magic. She was in what I would call a steroid honeymoon; new enough to the drug that she has no side-effects. That is, if you discount her almost manic ebullience and unfettered random energy. What's more, she has not gained weight, yet.

"Dr. Radis and Sandi! How good of you to stop by! Kate, you are indescribably beautiful! Turn around! Oh my! And Molly! Though I wish your parents had the good sense to dress you as a cat instead of a dog, you are sleeping which is the way I like my dogs. Come in! Come in!"

I waved my mom and Izzy inside and our extended family sipped on cups of hot cider. Lois exclaimed that she had so much energy from the prednisone she'd cleaned the cottage three times in the past two days. "The medicine makes me feel better than I deserve. The pain, the stiffness, the headaches have melted away. It was, she declared, a "miraculous miracle." As we prepared to leave, Lois bent down to show Kate the stitches on her left forehead from the temporal artery biopsy before flourishing her wand and dubbing Kate, "an official princess in good standing."

Next door was Elaine Quigg, considerably older than Lois, but perhaps, even more bustling and energetic. This was Elaine's natural state. I hadn't seen Elaine as a patient because she took no medications. Legally blind, with coke-bottle glasses, Elaine leaned in to take a closer look at the girls. "These costumes are homemade! Sandi? Did you sew these outfits?"

Sandi was pleased that Elaine recognized her work, perhaps even more so now that she was often referred to as the quirky lady plumber. "I had a few odds and ends, that's all," she said proudly. "It didn't take long. No reason to spend a lot when they're just going to outgrow their outfits."

Kate tugged at my coat. "Can we go to the spooky house?" In response, I lifted my arms and lurched outside in the direction of Scott and Nancy Nash, the first family of Peaks Island spookiness. The Nash's commitment to Halloween drama ran so deep they invited their Boston theater friends to participate. This year's theme was *The Lobsters Are in Charge.*

On the front lawn was a wondrous scene: magicians and sorcerers with glowing orbs, fishmongers and lobstermen in hip boots warning trick-or-treaters, *Go Back! Beware the lobster!* Kate squeezed my hand and inched her way forward. We ascended the creaky porch. Through the picture window a giant lobster sporting a jaunty white chef's hat stirred a gigantic pot. Suddenly, a young child emerged from the paper mache water and screamed, "Help me! Help me!" before the lid was slammed shut by the lobster chef.

I looked back. Molly was still asleep in Sandi's arms. Aunt Izzy and my mother parked the car and crossed the lawn, joining us on the porch. Kate's friend fled. "Look!" Aunt Izzy pointed, "A sign on the front door! They want us to go inside!" A true West Virginian, Aunt Izzy—afraid of absolutely nothing, real or imagined—grabbed my mother's elbow and disappeared inside. Coming to the end of the hallway, there was an open-mouthed gigantic clown face hung on the door with the command: *Collect your surprise. If you dare!* Izzy rolled up her coat sleeve and reached deep into the clown mouth.

At that moment, an accomplice, beneath an adjacent table, grabbed Aunt Izzy's ankle. Izzy shrieked and reflexively whammed the hand with her purse before falling heavily on her hip. In an instant, Izzy's true identity was clear. This wasn't a 10-year-old dressed up as an elderly woman, this was a 78-year-old lady dressed as an elderly woman.

The actor panicked. He lurched upward, nearly knocking himself out beneath the table. Crawling out from beneath the table on all fours, he sobbed, "I'm so sorry! I'm so sorry! Oh my gosh, are you hurt? Are you hurt?" For a moment, silence. Then Aunt Izzy erupted into a sniffling, snorting, uncontrolled howl. Still laughing, she pushed herself to her feet, marched in place, and declared she was just fine. My mother couldn't help herself. She peed in her pants. Just a little.

That was enough excitement for my mom and Aunt Izzy. They walked back to their car. Kate's friend appeared out of nowhere and the two compared candy hauls. Kate whispered to me, "Dad, Nicole says that the nuns have the best candy. Can we go see the nuns?"

"Honey, the Saint Joseph's retirement home is too far away. Your mother and I—"

At that moment, Izzy, her hand on the steering wheel, rolled down her window and yelled, "Chuck, do you know where the nuns live?" Evidently the word on the street was that the nun's retirement home was awash in candy.

We crowded into the backseat, Molly on Sandi's lap, Kate on my lap, friend Nicole pinned between Izzy and my mother. As Izzy turned on the ignition, Sandi tapped her on the shoulder. "Izzy, Chuck is too big for the back seat. Can he drive?" Reluctantly, Izzy switched places. It was well known on Peaks that Izzy, at under five feet tall, was a menace on the road. Although she and my mother had been on the island less than twenty-four hours, Izzy had already backed up and knocked over a mailbox. Putting me in the driver's seat was pure Sandi.

St. Joseph's by the Sea Catholic retirement home, where the nuns reside, was less than a mile away. On Peaks Island, most everything is less than a mile away. As we pulled in, I noticed the nuns' cream-colored van was parked in the gravel driveway slightly askew. Beneath the front right wheel was a flattened rhododendron. I noted this because I knew for a fact that among the six nuns not one possessed a valid driver's license. Last evening, Aunt Izzy and the nuns may have passed each other on Island Avenue—a sobering thought.

A light was on in the living room. The kids grabbed their trick or treat bags and rang the bell. Sister Mia opened the door and ushered Kate and Nicole inside for hot chocolate. "And you!" Sister Mia squinted in our direction. "Stop skulking about in the car. Come inside!"

Sister Mia held the door as we crossed the street and entered the foyer. I unzipped my down vest and laid Molly—who was still asleep—on a cushion on the floor. Behind the door, on a sturdy side table, was the biggest bowl of Snickers bars, M&Ms, Kit-Kats, and Hershey's bars on the planet. Sister Mia instructed the children to scoop out as much as their two hands could hold, "but that's all," as if this were a strict limitation. I raised an eyebrow but was quickly handed two Snickers bars. "Thank you."

I asked Sister Mia if I could use their bathroom. She pointed down a darkened hallway. On my way back, I passed Sister Marie Henry, who pulled me aside and whispered, "I think you would want to know; Sister Mia is off her diet." Then, in a conspiratorial tone she added, "Look to the left as you pass her bedroom. I'm not asking you to enter, just take a peek." Curious, I stuck my head into the next open doorway. On the nightstand was the second largest bowl of candy I'd ever seen. On the rumpled bed, more evidence; a semicircle of candy wrappers littered the sheets.

Sandi gathered Molly up and said it was getting late and time for bed. "For me," she added. As we silently filed out, Sister Mia lightly touched my shoulder and pointed to the knee I recently injected. "Thank you. It's better, definitely better." Outside, in the glow of a streetlight I wrote in my pocket calendar, *How do you solve a problem like Sister Mia?*

Our household slept fitfully that night on a sugar high. That is, Kate and I slept fitfully. Sandi, who demonstrates self-control and consumed a single Hershey's chocolate bar, and Molly, who for another year will eat what her mother tells her to eat, slept like the dead. In the morning, a Saturday, I remembered Bobby Emerson could use some help pulling his lobster boat. Between an unforgiving northeast wind and unfavorable tides, he'd held off pulling the *Carrie Anne*. This morning, the bay was flat and calm. Today was the day.

Lacing up my boots after breakfast, I flushed a dozen deer from the alder thicket on my way to the truck. Not so many years ago, the animals kept to the deeper, undisturbed woods of the island's interior. I might go the better part of a year and not see a single deer. When I did, my encounter was often limited to a flashing white tail bounding into the underbrush. Now they are everywhere.

Deer fences—eight feet high at the minimum—were going up everywhere. Sprays containing rotten eggs, garlic, and chili peppers were ineffective. Of course, it didn't help that several families had recently established winterfeeding stations in their backyards for the deer. The buck feeding on the Friedman's candle-lit pumpkin was only the latest example of their brazen, domesticated behavior.

Peaks is part of the city of Portland, and hunting is forbidden within city limits. Starting up my truck, I wondered if the spread of Lyme disease onto the Casco Bay Islands might be the tipping point for a hunt. So far, the only cases of Lyme disease I'd diagnosed had been contracted on the mainland, but it was only a matter of time before the deer tick spreads to Peaks, if it hadn't already.

After grabbing a cup of coffee at Lisa's I parked my truck at the base of the Army Pier. The next ferry will arrive in about an hour. If all went well, today would be an easy day at the hospital. Between catching up on my medical records and seeing three patients, I should be home on the 12:15 ferry from town.

I watched Bobby Emerson maneuver the *Carrie Anne* in close to shore. On the previous low tide, he'd used a tractor to drag his boat cradle down the sloping sand beach from where it sat against the hillside. Bobby cut the engine, tied off the bow to the submerged cradle and clambered into his dinghy. With the outgoing tide, the boat would settle, and the boat and cradle would then be winched above the high tide until next spring.

On the beach was Rick Crowley. His boat, *E Cosi*, bobbed on a mooring a hundred yards offshore. Rick's busy season was coming up. In January, the scallop season opens. Until the state scallop quota was reached, Rick would drag for scallops from dawn to dusk with his wife Nancy in the relatively shallow waters of Casco Bay. Rick paced on the shore, waiting for Bobby to row in. He was a bundle of barely restrained energy as he readied a walkway of heavy planks to pull the *Carrie Anne* shoreward.

They didn't need me, but I walked down anyway. "Hey Rick, nearly done?"

Rick stopped for a moment and shook my hand. I'm dressed for work and his restless blue eyes rove from me to Bobby to the cable attached to the cradle. He wears a black wool watch cap, an unzipped jacket, and a t-shirt. His jeans are tucked into a pair of sturdy Grunden insulated boots. "You missed the excitement, Bobby almost tipped out of his punt a minute ago. But, hey, he's in shallow water. If he falls in, he can probably stand up." As he spoke, Rick stooped to pick up a thick oak board from the underbrush and recoiled like he'd been bit by a snake. "Sh--t!" Blood dripped off his fingers and stained his jeans. He wrapped a rag around the hand and stooped down for a closer look at the board. "Great, some douchebag dumped a bunch of sea glass on the board."

"Here, let me take a look."

Rick hesitated for a moment, then extended his hand. I slowly unwrapped the rag. A gaping laceration ran along his index finger. The digital artery was spared. In an ideal world, the wound could use four or five stitches.

"You could use a few stitches," I said.

"I'm fine. Got any Steri-Strips?"

"Up in the truck. Sure you don't want me to open the health center?"

"Nah. No health insurance. I'll be fine."

I went up to the truck and pulled out my First-Aid kit from the glove compartment. Returning to the beach, I dabbed the finger in iodine before pulling the wound together with several Steri-Strips and wrapped it with a protective bandage. I looked up from my work and saw the *Machigonne* ferry emptying out on the adjacent wharf.

"What do I owe you?" Rick had his wallet out.

"We're good," I replied. "I have a few patients I need to round on at the hospital. See you around." I turned and gathered up my materials. "There is one thing. I'm curious about scalloping. Any chance I can join you and Nancy sometime this winter?"

Rick looked past me, out to his boat. "Between the scallop bar and by-catch, the deck is slick as sh--t. I don't know. I'll think about it."

"I'll check in sometime in January."

"You do that."

Onboard the *Machigonne*, I settled onto a green wooden bench in the hold and opened a boating magazine. As I thumbed through the pages, I stopped. Hmm . . . this was interesting. C-Dory, Small—only sixteen feet, but with a cuddy cabin. I flipped to the next page. High gunnels, but relatively flat bottom. On the stern was a fifty-horsepower Suzuki. That should be economical. A couple of seats inside the cuddy cabin to duck out of the wind or rain or snow. Good. I flipped to the next page. The boat plus trailer and motor had a suggested retail price of $13,000. Maybe.

I curled the page and tossed it back in my green satchel, then zipped up my hood and took the stairs to the top deck. We were passing Fort Gorges. The flat-bottomed keel of a C-Dory would be perfect to pull up at Fort Gorges on an incoming tide. I envisioned myself on the C-Dory; exploring the bay on a rare day off. Captain Chuck.

As we turned the corner at the Maine State Pier, I scanned across the inner harbor. Except for several tugs and the Coast Guard buoy tender, the bay was deserted. Off our bow, a flock of long-tail ducks scattered toward deeper water. I scribbled a note in my pocket calendar to find out the derivation of their former, politically incorrect name: Old-squaw. Two chunky male eiders poked around the rotting pilings diving for mussels, a primary food source. Herring gulls, now gathering in flocks of several hundred—a prelude to winter breeding—rode out the deeper swells coming in from Portland Head Light.

My hand wandered into my front left pocket for my keys. Shoot! No car keys. I rifled through my satchel. Don't panic. Then it came to me, they were in my pants I took off and threw in the laundry hamper. And because this had happened maybe four times in the last six months, I remembered there was now a spare key in a magnetic container inside the rear bumper of the intown car. That's progress, kind of.

59

The morning flew by. I discharged several patients and tentatively promised a Chebeague Island patient that if her orbital cellulitis infection continued to improve, we could switch over to oral antibiotics later today and discharge her in the morning. "In time for the 11:15 ferry?" she asked. In response, I calculated the time and distance to the ferry landing and wrote in my pocket calendar: *Discharge Chebeague patient before 10 tomorrow.* After dictating a half-dozen discharge summaries, I dropped by the doctors' dining room for a cup of coffee. Alone with my thoughts I opened up the newspaper and felt myself relax.

An orthopedic surgeon I regularly referred patients to came through the door with his lunch tray and wanted to talk about a malpractice claim that had gone on for two years and was still unresolved.

It had begun with an evaluation in the emergency room at three in the morning. The surgeon was called in to see a young man who'd suffered a fractured hip in a motorcycle accident. The surgeon spent an hour picking out gravel and pieces of shredded jeans imbedded in the wound before he pinned the hip. Infection at the operative site occurred a week later and required a prolonged hospitalization. Within six months, the femoral head, which fits into the hip socket, crumpled due to avascular necrosis (dead bone). A total hip replacement was performed. The patient could no longer work as a mechanic. Not long after, a malpractice suit was delivered to the orthopedic surgeon's office.

As he spoke, the surgeon's eyes welled up and his voice dropped to a whisper. I listened quietly, aware that I was hearing a selective telling of the particulars of the story, but also knowing that cases such as this were always complicated. All I knew was that this particular surgeon did good work, my patients liked him, and he was respected by his peers.

The surgeon was angry, not just at the patient and his lawyer, but at the snail's pace of the proceedings. "I've held out. No way was I going to settle. The trial finally starts Tuesday." He drained the last of his coffee and stood quietly for a moment. "I'm not sleeping. I can't concentrate. It can't end soon enough."

"I'm sorry." I extended a hand. "Everyone knows you're a good surgeon. You take great care of your patients." What I didn't say was that several years ago I'd also been sued. He was reaching out and I failed to share my own painful experience.

After he left, I nursed the last of my coffee and thought back to the day my world turned upside down. A middle-age garbage worker had consulted me at my intown office. He was the brother of a Peaks Island patient and was concerned about a vague aching beneath his breastbone while emptying cans into the truck. If he paced himself or lifted lighter loads, he was okay. The chest pressure was occurring with less and less exertion; he wondered if it was his heart.

He had the full house for risk factors: Overweight and a heavy smoker, his blood pressure and fasting cholesterol were markedly elevated. I suggested a treadmill and several days later, put him through his paces. His chest pressure recurred at a low level of exercise. The EKG tracings clearly showed that his symptoms were due to coronary artery disease.

I prescribed a betablocker for his hypertension, twice daily long-acting nitroglycerin to improve blood flow through the narrowed coronary arteries, convinced him to follow a cholesterol lowering diet, and prescribed an aspirin to thin his blood. Then I wrote a note to temporarily keep him out of work and made an appointment in ten days for a repeat treadmill. That's when I made my first mistake; I scribbled down my findings and recommendations in his chart. It was a brief note, too brief.

When he arrived for his repeat treadmill, my patient's blood pressure was much improved. He told me that he'd cut "way back" on cigarettes, improved his diet, and was anxious to return to work. During the past ten days there had been no further bouts of angina. And the treadmill was definitely improved. I pushed him relatively hard, and the EKG didn't demonstrate a heart-strain pattern until the very end, when he broke into a jog.

I wrote another prescription, this time clearing him for work, but only as a driver, and again, jotted a brief note. A week later I was notified that my patient had dropped dead at work. He left a wife and two teenage children. Several months later, a letter from the family's lawyer arrived in the mail. I was accused of malpractice. That evening I brought the chart home and pored over it after dinner. There were gaps in the record. I *thought* I had recommended that the patient undergo a heart catheterization, but that he'd refused and wanted to try the medicines first. I was *sure* that I recommended that he quit smoking—I always recommend that patients quit smoking—but again, my hand-written note didn't reflect this.

In the ensuing weeks and months, the discrepancy between my memory and the written notes disrupted my sleep and affected my mood. I toggled between compassion and sorrow for my patient and his family and the belief that I had done nothing wrong. Or had I? What if I'd never told him that a cardiac catheterization might lead to open-heart surgery and a bypass of the diseased arteries? What if I never mentioned he should quit cigarettes? To deal with the additional stress hanging over me, Sandi pushed me out of the house for late evening runs around the island. I wrestled and played with the kids. I tried to limit alcohol to one beer each evening but wasn't always successful.

One morning I picked up the phone and called a psychologist who specialized in hypnosis. Perhaps under hypnosis I could determine what my true memories were. I cleared out a morning of office visits and reported, with some trepidation, to the therapist's office. Yes, she'd be glad to perform hypnosis, but first she needed to get a better sense of who I was, what made me tick. Her questioning focused on events long before my encounter with the cardiac patient, to my childhood, to the death of my father. She wanted to understand me. I wanted to deal with the present. After three visits, I'd had enough. We were at cross-purposes; I wanted to know whether my memories were accurate, she wanted to know how the loss of my father at an early age affected my present work. I canceled our next session and never went back.

In Maine, medical malpractice suits are initially brought before a screening panel. A retired judge, a psychologist, and a minister served on mine. When the Maine legislature created the panel, the goal was to reduce the number of cases requiring a jury trial. And for the most part, the system worked. In cases where the panel unanimously agreed that malpractice occurred, doctors often settle rather than risk a larger judgement from a sympathetic jury. On the other hand, if the panel finds there was no malpractice, the suit is often dropped. Malpractice jury trials (which the surgeon was scheduled for), were reserved for only the most contentious, controversial cases.

My screening panel "trial" lasted two days. Surprisingly, the lawyer for the family didn't question me about my sparse notes or ask why I hadn't referred the patient for a coronary angiogram. The focus was on why I returned the patient to work with known heart disease and why a cardiologist wasn't consulted. Two cardiologists were called as expert witnesses; one testified that he would have prescribed the same medications and that it was perfectly appropriate for internists to manage heart disease, the other testified that my care was substandard. Sitting through the testimony was a low point in my medical career.

What seemed to influence the panel the most, however, were the details—previously unknown to me—of exactly what happened to my patient. My lawyer explained that his demise occurred when the crew stopped for a break. He was smoking when he suddenly keeled over and died. He could have, my lawyer argued, died at home or driving his car. There was no autopsy. His sudden death could have been due to a heart attack, or alternatively, a pulmonary embolism, a cardiac arrhythmia, or a massive stroke, none of which could have been predicted or prevented based on the evidence.

The panel voted 3-0 that malpractice was not responsible for my patient's death. The suit was settled. I did not have the sword of Damocles hanging over me, as the poor orthopedic surgeon did, endlessly awaiting a jury trial.

Back on the ferry, heading home to Peaks, my mind drifted back to the simple question, *was I good doctor?* What other mistakes had I made in my four years in practice? An internist's practice is more difficult to judge than a surgeon's, whose complications are often glaringly obvious: an instrument left in the belly; an operation on the wrong foot; a post-op complication due to inattentiveness.

I asked myself once again, *was I a good doctor?*

I opened my pocket calendar and made several rough calculations. Last year, between my clinic days on Chebeague and Peaks Islands, rounds at the osteopathic hospital, and my part-time practice in Portland, I had three-thousand patient visits. Of course, many of these were routine with little likelihood for error. For example, in newly recognized hypertension, there are widely recognized guidelines for treatment. In strep throat, the streptococcus bacteria is uniformly sensitive to penicillin. More complex cases, where signs and symptoms require a work-up, are ripe for misdiagnosis or improper management.

Lack of follow-up is where patients are most at risk for poor outcomes, and where physicians are justifiably sued. Culture reports return and antibiotics are not adjusted for resistant organisms. Test results are not discussed or missed altogether. This was why I wrote down reminders in my pocket calendar as I pinballed between my various practice settings. Sometimes I wrote down reminders about reminders.

Practicing outside the scope of your training or comfort zone is a recipe for poor outcomes. Some of my island patients balk when I suggest a referral to a specialist in Portland. Some would rather not leave the island at all. Since my lawsuit, when a patient refuses a referral and insists that I manage their case, I'd been more careful to document this in my note.

Then there are unexpected deaths. This may or may not be due to poor decision making. Just as bad things happen to good people, sometimes bad results occur despite a correct diagnosis and skilled management. The head of my internal medicine program, Dr. Phil Slocum, once told me, "You haven't been in practice long enough if you haven't killed a patient." At the time his advice sounded harsh, but I understood now what he was trying to say. Of my 3,000 patient visits per year, if my decision making was correct on 99% of those visits, potentially, that left thirty wrong decisions per year. Make that 99.9% and three wrong decisions remain. Some of those decisions have minimal consequences, but sooner or later, a poor decision, an overlooked laboratory study or pathology report has a major effect on a patient's outcome.

Several years ago, I performed a house call on an elderly woman on Peaks Island I had diagnosed with influenza. I began her on acyclovir, an effective treatment for the influenza virus, and the diagnosis was confirmed by a nasal swab. Influenza is a serious, sometimes life-threatening illness, particularly in the elderly, so I dropped by her house two days later and listened to her chest and looked her over. She was still weak, but her fever was down, and her appetite improved.

Several days after my visit, she arose in the morning and walked to the bathroom, collapsed, and died. A neighbor found her a few hours later. An autopsy demonstrated an unusual finding. Her lungs were sparsely involved by the virus, but there was fluid surrounding the heart, a pericardial effusion. The case weighed heavily on me. Why didn't I recognize that she had a life-threatening complication of influenza? Should I have admitted her to the hospital? I wondered, rightly or wrongly, if I had listened more closely to her heart, would I have called the fireboat and transferred her to the hospital. But perhaps not. Perhaps the fluid accumulated so rapidly, there was nothing to recognize on the day I'd last seen her. I'd never know.

The *Machigonne* slowed for the approach to Peaks. Coming in hard, the ferry bumped the wharf before the crew secured the fore and aft lines. The gangplank clanged as it was pushed shoreward and tied off. Trudging up the hill, I was grateful that the wind was at my back, the pale late fall sun floating over the distant Portland skyline. A flock of crows harassed a Canada goose on the beach until it flapped angrily into the shallows beneath the pier. Bobby Emerson's boat was tucked in for the winter above the high-tide line on the sandy beach. On upside-down lobster crates, Rick and Bobby pointed beers in my direction. I looked at my watch; it wouldn't hurt to say hello.

8

The week before Christmas, a nor-easter funneled up the coast, brushed the tip of Cape Cod, and plowed into southern Maine. The city of Portland lost power for the better part of a day. On Peaks, the power plant next door to us came online and electricity was restored in less than an hour.

Thanks to the power plant, when the lights go out in Portland, Peaks glows brightly across the bay. During the 1920s, the plant burned coal and produced gas as a byproduct. The gas was piped to lamps lining a boardwalk and each evening, an employee of the power plant walked his enormous pet pig along the boardwalk lighting each gas lamp with a long pole.

The boardwalk and gas lamps are long gone and today, the power plant is powered by oil. A swampy moat surrounds the base of the oil tank, and there is an upside to this. In May, spring peepers awaken from the mud (a specialized blood antifreeze helps the inch-long frogs survive the winter); their chirping evening chorus is a welcome harbinger of spring and the greening of the island.

In the morning, I tried to shovel out our truck on the edge of the road, but the snowplow had already come by and splayed icy chunks of ice and snow against the driver's door. I grabbed my backpack and green satchel and headed off to clinic. With each storm, the snowbanks on the edge of the road rise higher and higher. How high? As I approached the school, I noticed the word *car* spray-painted in foot-high blue letters on a suspicious mound. A deer ambled across the road ahead of me, then two more darted across. With the heavy snow, the deer were moving out of their winter yard in the middle of the island to browse on shrubs and low trees next to year-round homes

We now had skunks on Peaks Island. Coming home from a recent evening house-call, I came across a pair tearing apart a garbage bag on

Luther Street. How did the skunks arrive on Peaks? There's a rumor that Long Island lobstermen live-trapped a half-dozen skunks (the animals won't spray unless they have room to lift their tail) and dropped them off on Peaks in the middle of the night as payback in a long-running feud with several local lobstermen.

After stamping the snow off my boots in the entranceway of the health center, I strode briskly through the waiting room and nodded hello to Sister Mia. Johnny Dinsmore, the janitor for the Peaks Island school, unzipped his light jacket and settled into a chair. Johnny's face contorted as he removed his boot and ever so gently placed his foot up on a stool. Gout? I wondered. Anne handed him a cane and ushered him into an exam room, but not before he extended his hand in my direction and repeated his favorite line, "Shake the hand of the man who shook the hand of the man who shook the hand of Lincoln's." I did the math. It was possible.

Then I addressed the mess on my desk. Lab slips and radiology reports poked out here and there amidst a stack of charts. A recent copy of the *New England Journal of Medicine* lay open, book marked to a review article on temporal arteritis.

Anne had not given up, yet, on her efforts to organize me. My wife Sandi chose to work around the edges, preferring that I suffer consequences for my forgetfulness. It was my problem, not Sandi's problem. Anne had a different approach. She started with a simple *in* and *out* wooden box on my desk. I used this for a day, then ignored it, or, more specifically, I used it sparingly before creating a third, unnamed pile that was neither *in* nor *out*. Items in this pile I'd reviewed, but required more information before I could make a final decision.

Then Anne taped a paper to the wall above the left side of my desk and wrote: Important papers *here*, with an arrow pointing down. The space lay fallow. Next, came an attempt at a bulletin board, then a file cabinet. Neither held much interest for me.

This, this pile of stuff, I suspected, was not where my life went sideways. Despite the consequences of missed information, my mind sifted through a mountain of data in its own mysterious fashion. For one, it helped that I remember the results of tests. It seems to reside in a particular part of my brain, entirely separate from my . . . what . . .

forgetfulness lobe? If I read a disturbing report or lab value it pushes forward into my consciousness until I do something about it. I may be pouring myself a cup of coffee or visiting the bathroom or walking to clinic or eating lunch when I find myself writing a sticky pad list of tasks or adding an entry to my pocket planner. And generally, I know where the information is in that stack of papers. I have no idea how or why.

If there is one adjustment I'd made, it was comprehensively documenting my visits. Before my malpractice suit, I scribbled or dictated a brief note. The note was primarily for me, not for a lawyer or jury. There was just enough documentation to successfully manage the patient at a follow-up visit. Now, my notes were more extensive and comprehensive. I was careful to add disclaimers: *Patient missed an appointment with dermatology for suspicious mole.* Or, *Suggest mammogram, patient wants to wait.*

Inside the exam room, Johnny's big toe was warm and swollen. I knew from past encounters that the toe would "hurt a mite," but the word *pain* is not in the Irishman's vocabulary. This is remarkable in that gout is one of the most painful afflictions in medicine. No one has captured the suffering of gout as vividly as Dr. Thomas Sydenham (himself a gout sufferer), who wrote in 1673, *The victim goes to bed and sleeps in good health. About 2 o'clock in the morning, he is awakened by a severe pain in the great toe . . . This pain is like that of a dislocation, and yet the parts feel as if cold water were poured over them. The pain which is at first moderate becomes more intense. Now it is a violent stretching and tearing of the ligaments– now it is a gnawing pain and now a pressure and tightening. So exquisite and lively meanwhile is the feeling of the part affected, that it cannot bear the weight of bedclothes nor the jar of a person walking in the room.*

To be absolutely sure that the swelling in Johnny's big toe represented gout, joint aspiration, followed by analysis of the fluid for uric acid crystals was often performed. And there were times when I aspirated a puzzling joint. But not today. The diagnostic possibilities for his swollen toe were gout, gout, and gout. No, it was really a management problem. Johnny would willingly ingest the indomethacin I doled out to bring the current attack under control. After all, he could barely fit his foot into his boot. It was the prevention of future attacks where we were falling short.

I asked him, "Are you taking your daily allopurinol I prescribed?"

"No," he shrugged, "Should I be?"

I resisted the urge to whack myself on the forehead. We'd had this conversation before. Allopurinol must be taken daily, and the dose slowly titrated upward until the uric acid level drops into the normal range. And there are patients, compliant patients, who find that year after year, they are gout free . . . as long as they take the pill. There are others who run out, forget to take, or stop allopurinol for no apparent reason. Johnny was of this ilk. Some patients simply out-drink the drug. Alcoholics, notably, simply defy successful management for gout.

For today's misery, I gave Johnny samples of indomethacin and asked him to return in a week. As an afterthought, I wrote out a reminder: *Take ALLOPURINOL every day*, and asked him to tape it to the refrigerator door.

As I exited the exam room, I nearly bumped into Sister Mia standing glumly on the scale. Next to her was a large paper bag. Stepping off the scale, she picked up the bag, and held it tightly against her chest as she followed Anne into the exam room. A few minutes later, Anne emerged, and with her now familiar red magic marker, circled Sister Mia's blood pressure. Peering over her glasses, she said, "Sister Mia has a confession to make. It's in the bag."

Not a moment after I closed the door, Sister Mia thrust the paper bag onto me, and declared she was done with candy. Done. "Take them away. Get them from my sight!" I peered into the bag and suppressed a smile. Loose M&Ms, Kit-Kat bars, Milky Ways, loose candy corn, marshmallow snowmen, and a Twinkie gleamed like pirate's loot, in all their high-caloric glory. Amongst this diabetic minefield, a single banana floated like a canoe, swept up in Sister Mia's decision to come clean.

But I was also aware that Sister Mia was more than the sum of her daily calories and struggle with diabetes. Countless islanders turned to her for advice and spiritual support. Notably, she stayed in touch with a young man who had been sexually abused on the island. Her constant devotion and friendship no doubt played a role in his recovery.

But even as a rock for others, she likely carried her own scars and emotional injuries. I wondered what led her into the sisterhood in the first place? Was it solely for a life of service to God and her community? Or was her decision, in part, a reflection of her own difficult upbringing and an escape from her family? As her doctor, I knew so little about her. I wondered who knew her story.

I retook Sister Mia's blood pressure and it remained ominously high. Despite her outward serenity, her forehead glistened with sweat. "Last night," she leaned in, "I had an . . . event. I was writing a letter and I dropped my pen and couldn't speak. I tried to cry out but the words spilled out in gibberish. By the time Sister Marie-Henry came running into the room, it had passed."

"Why didn't you call? If I'd known, I would have sent for the fireboat, I—"

"There will be no fireboat."

I rubbed my forehead, sorting out the next step. Then I reached into the cabinet and opened a sample of lisinopril. "Let's start you on this new blood pressure medication. Take it with your other blood pressure meds."

"What *other* blood pressure medications?" she asked, as she swallowed the lisinopril.

I ignored this, took a deep breath, and slowly exhaled. Was anyone on this island following my advice? I placed my stethoscope lightly over Sister Mia's neck and listened to the carotid arteries. On the left, the opposite side of her clumsy hand episode last night, was a rumbling *shhhhh*, synchronous with each beat of her heart. Carotid stenosis. Last night, under high pressure, a fragment had broken off and traveled upstream and lodged into a small branch of the middle cerebral artery, temporarily blocking a portion of her brain controlling speech and the function of her right hand. It was an ominous sign. I flipped through her chart and found an ultrasound report of the carotids from several years ago. There was narrowing, but not to the point where surgical intervention was indicated. Now that Sister Mia had experienced her first transient ischemic attack (TIA), we need to relook at the carotid narrowing again. It was likely she'd require surgery—an endarterectomy, but first I'd redouble my efforts at normalizing her blood pressure. I asked Sister Mia to sit in the waiting room while I saw the remainder of my morning patients.

Despite her fifteen-pound weight gain, Lois Herndon was "fabulous." The muscle stiffness and headaches had resolved. A recent erythrocyte sedimentation rate (ESR) was, reassuringly, in the normal range and I instructed her to reduce the prednisone from 60 mg daily to 40. She was nearly out the door, when I called her back, "One more thing, long-term prednisone can lead to osteoporosis. I need to schedule you for a bone density test in Portland. In the meantime, if you haven't started a calcium and vitamin D supplement, please do." Lois dutifully wrote down my recommendation and placed it in her purse. Thank you, Lois.

An elderly woman came in focused on her constipation. A five-year-old was brought in by her mother with an itchy rash. I tested a teenager, home from school for a third day with a sore throat, for both strep and mononucleosis. The tests were negative, but I drew a CBC; she looked pale and washed out. During a lull, I discussed Sister Mia's event with a vascular surgeon while Anne arranged for an ultrasound of the carotid arteries and an MRI scan of the head in Portland. I was in luck; the surgeon agreed to see her the next afternoon, review the scans, and decide if she was a candidate for surgery.

Sister Mia's repeat blood pressure was 148/88. Not great, but good enough. Sister Marie-Henry drove Sister Mia home, but not before she clipped the edge of the handicap ramp with the front fender. As she backed up onto Sterling Street, the wheels spun on a patch of black ice and the van narrowly missed a parked car. It was ironic that even as Sister Mia's risk of stroke had diminished, her risk of serious injury with Sister Marie-Henry at the wheel might have landed her on the fireboat.

On my way to the ferry, I purchased a cup of coffee at Lisa's and decided not to add a plastic lid to the cup. Lisa noticed—she notices everything—and said, "That coffee is hot," as in, *why in heavens name are you walking to the ferry with an open cup of coffee?* I answered that the lid was plastic. It would end up in the dump or in the bay. Why not carefully balance the coffee and sip on it without the need for a lid? If some of the coffee splashes out, I'd do a better job next time. Call me lidless.

Picking my way down the hill, I boarded the *Machigonne* without mishap, and tucked in behind the pilot house. My beeper vibrated and I glanced at the number. It can wait. I exhaled, sipped on my coffee, and felt my shoulders relax. Approaching Portland, the *Machigonne* plowed through a field of ice at the entrance to the inner harbor. This time of year, car-sized slabs flowed down from the Fore River. It would take a prolonged cold snap before the ice extended as a continuous sheet into the harbor.

There was something in or on the water. Coming closer, I saw it was a harbor seal that had pulled itself up on the ice, its weight dragging the small ice slab under water, producing the surreal effect of the seal magically suspended on the surface. As if sensing my disbelief, the seal arched its back before sliding gracefully into the black water.

After rounding on several patients at the hospital, I drove up the coast to the Chebeague ferry landing. For once, I was early; across the channel the ferry was pushing off from the Chebeague side. I wandered down to the wharf and glanced at the miniature L.L. Bean thermometer attached to my zipper: 11 degrees. A patch of sea smoke rimmed the bay. As a lobster boat idled down to approach the dock, a razorbill (a seagull-sized relative of the puffin), surfaced just off the stern. In a panic, the black and white bird submerged so quickly, I was unsure exactly what I'd seen. A minute later, the bird resurfaced in deeper water, bobbing like a cork.

The lobster boat tied off, and it was Ben Shipman, my rheumatoid arthritis patient picking up his wife, Laurie, from town. I hitched a ride.

Ben seemed to be moving well as we cast off. The boat was freshly rigged for scalloping. Maneuvering into the channel, he sipped coffee out of a thermos and offered me a cup. The steaming coffee fogged up the windshield and Ben removed a mitten to wipe the glass. The knuckles on his right-hand were swollen, but improved from several months before. He slid off the other mitten and balanced his hands on the wheel. "I'm a good 50% better, maybe more, on the weekly methotrexate the rheumatologist prescribed. And the shots you gave me for my knees worked; they're fine. Can we go up on the methotrexate?"

"Yes. Stop by the clinic later this morning," I answered. "We need some follow-up labs to make sure the current dose is safe; sometimes the liver can be injured by the methotrexate and we can't increase the dose."

"I'll do that."

I learned more in the fifteen-minute trip to Chebeague about Ben's rheumatoid arthritis than in a dozen office visits. By wrapping the wheel in foam tubing, he now had a larger, more forgiving surface to maneuver his boat. Everything he needed in the wheelhouse was at hip level or higher. Crates and barrels were lighter and smaller. His marine radio's controls were changed out to larger, over-sized knobs. Still, his RA was not anywhere near remission. He was scalloping, but I could see it was still a struggle. Some patients with rheumatoid arthritis have a smoldering course with little or no damage over decades; Ben's fingers were already deviating away from his thumbs. We'd need to do better if he was to avoid early disability.

Tying off at the Stone Pier, I gathered my belongings and walked toward the parking lot. Albion waved to me from his seat near the window of the store. I started the engine of my borrowed Ford truck, and Albion wandered outside. "Think I'll drop by later today for a chat; the medicine seems to be helping. I wonder if we might go up on the dose a dite?"

Nothing like open-air office visits. Two of my favorite patients were on the mend. On the way to clinic, I noticed a snowy owl on a low branch in a white pine. As the bird flew off, I hit a patch of ice and the truck swerved. I overcorrected, and the truck dropped into a shallow ditch paralleling the road. I slammed my hand on the wheel. That was stupid. I rocked the truck back and forth but no use—I was stuck.

Albion came by in his truck and was sympathetic and annoyingly cheerful. My accident could have happened to most anyone, he insisted. Then he attached a chain from the bumper of his truck to my front bumper and pulled me out. "You ain't the first to go off the road here; that snowy owl is catching most everybody's eye."

Arriving at the clinic, I wondered how long my mishap would remain a secret. Probably about twenty minutes. Clinic hours were light. I was slowly adjusting to the fact that on the islands, many well-off, older, year-round residents migrated south for the winter. Some of these folks were my sickest, frailest patients who I saw regularly. I didn't notice the phenomenon as much on Peaks, where there's a large enough population to keep me busy through the winter. But the flip side is also true; come summer, between the return of elderly year-round islanders and the influx of summer residents, I was flat out from dawn to dusk and beyond.

Back home early, I walked the beach with Sandi as Kate and Molly clambered onto ice chunks left by the receding tide. Our cat Isabel followed at a discreet distance. She was interested in watching us, but being a cat, didn't want to appear to be *that* interested. The children, dressed in boots and red snowsuits, dug up frozen sand and flung empty mussel and clam shells into the shallows. Across the channel, the down-the-bay ferry, the *Island Holiday*, chugged by, hugging the shore of Little Diamond Island.

I checked back on Isabel, and there she was, flattened like a rug, her front paws extended, the rear paws splayed out to the rear. A shadow passed overhead. It was a bald eagle, hoping to pick off a stray eider or pigeon or . . . cat. The eagle silently cruised the beach for another hundred yards before banking toward Fort Gorges. Being primarily an indoor cat, Isabel had probably never seen an eagle before, but instinct had kicked in when she spotted it, and it was some minutes before she rose up and silently padded back to the house.

That night the phone rang with the answering service forwarding me the number of the mother of a four-year-old I'd seen several days before with a viral upper respiratory tract infection. Tonight, her asthma was worse, much worse, and I suggested they meet me at the health center. When I arrived, mom was at the front door with Tanya, bundled up against the cold. I flipped on the lights in the front room. Tanya sat on her mother's lap and leaned slightly forward, laboring for air. Placing my stethoscope on her chest, high-pitched wheezes were audible throughout both lung fields. She looked scared.

Leaving them for a moment, I opened the lower cabinet where the emergency box was stored. Inside, was a yellow sticky pad note: *Replenish albuterol aerosol for emergency kit.* Next to it was the spare. Grabbing the remaining aerosol, I scribbled a second note, *Out of albuterol aerosol, buy 2 TODAY,* and placed it on Anne's seat. Before returning to the waiting room I dialed the police and asked them to call the fireboat.

Tanya looked up vacantly as I secured the aerosol nebulizer to her face before she settled back into her mother's arms. I wheeled in the oxygen tank and secured the plastic tubing around her ears before lightly pressing the soft prongs into her nose. The ambulance pulled up and I quietly opened the front entrance for Mike and Big John. Mike brought in an extra oxygen tank. Big John mentioned that the fireboat should be at the Public Safety float in about twenty minutes. In my shirt pocket was a syringe of epinephrine, a just-in-case treatment if the aerosol failed to break the attack.

Big John handed mom a storybook from the toy bin behind the front door. Over the course of fifteen minutes, Tanya's breathing became less labored. Her interest in the storybook picked up. That's the way it is with children; when they're sick, they're *really* sick, when they turn the corner, it's like nothing happened. By the time Tanya and her mother left the health center in the front seat of the ambulance, Tanya's asthma was remarkably improved.

At the fireboat, Tanya squirmed in her mother's arms and refused to wear the oxygen. One of the EMTs raised an eyebrow signaling, *We've been called on an emergency for this?* But I wasn't embarrassed; a flare of asthma is serious, and it's better to call for a transfer than second-guess whether the aerosol will work. At the very least, she and her mother should spend the night in town.

Parking the truck at the top of the walkway, I picked my way toward the house under a moonless sky, stepping lightly around patches of ice. Before opening the front door, I peered down to the beach, across the windless bay, to the glowing lights of Portland. The Milky Way floated overhead on a velvet carpet. A meteor sizzled downward, and then another. As my eyes adjusted to the blackness, I became aware of a faint, shimmering curtain extending from the northern horizon toward the Big Dipper. Over the next few minutes, hints of pink and polar blue spread across the horizon until a spectacular show lit up nearly the entire sky. In a few minutes, the only portion of sky without the dancing curtains of light was directly overhead, a black hole of sparkling stars.

Entering the house, I went directly upstairs to Molly's room. With her early bedtime, I often went several days without seeing her and the guilt I felt transformed to a deep longing. I quietly stood by her bed and picked her up. Her eyes remained closed, and I bundled her up and started down the stairs. Sandi cracked open our bedroom door, "Is Molly okay?"

"Yes, she's sleeping. I want to show her something."

"Chuck Radis, you are not bringing her outside on a night like this."

"I'll put a knit cap on her. She has to see this. You have to see this. I'll let Kate sleep; I think she's seen the aurora borealis before."

I wrapped Molly in a blanket and snugged a tiny knit cap over her head without awakening her. Outside, the sky was alive with shimmering columns of light, pointing upward as if the entire Earth were a beacon pointing toward a celestial destination. We stood there in silence, heads craned, leaning against the doorway. I whispered quietly to Molly that she was a lucky girl, that I was glad she was asleep, and I would tell her about this, someday, when she was older. Sandi allowed herself a half-smile and remarked I was a very strange husband, that it was time for bed, and was the little girl with asthma okay?

9

I t was mid-February and I enjoyed a rare weekend off from my island medical practice. Childhood friends Tux, Rudy, Bruce, George, and Rob arrived on the noon ferry and threw their gear into the back of my truck. We have camped and canoed together since junior high in the wilds of New Jersey (okay, it *seemed* wild). Later, we moved on to more challenging winter camping trips in the Shawangunks in New York and the White Mountains in New Hampshire. If winter camping taught us anything, it was how to suffer. Tonight, we would be camping on the back shore of Peaks Island.

Coming off the boat, Tux, the prepared one, reminded me that I should bring a sleeping bag liner for my winter sleeping bag. "The latest radio report says it's getting into the single numbers tonight, maybe lower." Tux placed his backpack gently in the truck bed and added, "and think about a second pair of gloves to wear under your mittens." My ears perked up. After more than a dozen winter camping trips, I listened to Tux. The man was Mr. Organized and believed in redundancy. In case your feet get soaked, have an extra pair of dry socks. Bring two knit caps, that sort of thing. Then there was Rudy's approach to winter camping: "I grabbed a lot of stuff and threw it into this box." Of course, it helped that Rudy carried an extra sixty pounds of insulation over his rounded 5-foot-7-inch frame. Rudy's nickname, Dancing Bear, suited him to a T. In winter, instead of hibernating, the man danced in the cold.

After stopping at my house to pick up a few items, I drove slowly around to the back shore and stopped the truck. Except for a few seasonal homes, the one-mile stretch of road running along the water was deserted. A faint mist hung over the water. It was low tide and the crash of waves against Whaleback ledge alternated with the hiss of backwash on the gravel beach. On the horizon was Half-Way Rock Lighthouse, marking a dangerous ledge for incoming ships. To the southeast, open ocean.

We unloaded a tarp and a clump of rope above the high-tide mark and collected driftwood to build a sweat lodge. Rudy stomped down the snow where we would erect the structure while George cleared out debris for a fire pit. "Sweat lodge, sweat lodge!" Rudy shouted as he did a little dance. "Check this out." He pointed toward the driftwood. "First, we make the teepee, no problem. Then we wrap the plastic around it and bury the edges in the snow. When the boulders glow red-hot in the outside fire, we roll them into the middle of the teepee."

"And then?" I asked.

"And then we add water. The steam rises from the red-hot boulders, curls around behind us, and slaps us in the back of the head. Freedom!"

We nodded our heads in agreement. What could possibly go wrong?

I looked behind us, across a frozen marsh, to the top of Battery Steele, tonight's camping destination. Okay, I thought to myself, am I naked inside the sweat lodge? I wasn't sure I wanted to know.

The six of us went to work. In no time, the teepee was up and wrapped in plastic. Bruce cut out an entrance flap for us to crawl through and lugged in several logs to sit on. Because Rudy was half-Finnish, he had the honor of picking out the sauna stones and nestled them into the base of the driftwood for the night's bonfire. There seemed to be a lot of moving parts to Rudy's plan, but it just might work.

We returned to the truck and drove over to Battery Steele. During World War II the fortification housed two 16-inch artillery guns to protect the North Atlantic Fleet in Casco Bay from German U-Boats. Our campsite was at the top of the deserted cement battery. Picking our way to the top of the forty-foot-high embankment, we set up our tents in a clearing facing the ocean. I tried to light my single-burner stove. The fuel was frozen. Rudy tossed me a working fuel cartridge, and in a few minutes, I was heating up a can of Dinty Moore stew. We shared a Tupperware container of mint brownies Sandi had packed for us. Like a farm family, we were acutely aware that Rudy would grab more than his share if we didn't act quickly. Too late, I got one, Rude got three.

The sun dropped behind a cloud. I unzipped my parka for a moment and slipped on my down vest. Though it took only a moment, I began to shiver.

Rudy signaled that it was "sweat lodge" time. We filled our pockets with beer cans and snacks and returned to the rocky beach. Although it was only four in the afternoon, the sun had set over Battery Steele and a damp, cold chill penetrated my parka. The bone-dry driftwood caught fire and we leaned in for warmth. Alcohol was consumed. A few strides away stood our makeshift sweat lodge.

Mars, closer to Earth than it would be for years, hovered on the eastern horizon and cast a faint shadow over the water. As the last glow on the western horizon faded, a steady, penetrating raw wind picked up off the water. Bruce, as pencil thin as Rudy was pleasingly plump, picked out the Big Dipper, and following the edge of the dipper, located the North Star. I tried, unsuccessfully, to teach the group how to tell time by the Big Dipper as it moved counter-clockwise around the North Star, but this involved not only a determination of the Dipper's current location, but an addition, a doubling, and then a subtraction. No one was particularly interested.

In a vain attempt to keep warm, Bruce ran in place and swung his arms in exaggerated jumping jacks. The man could run forever but standing still as the temperature plummeted was agony. For a while, the balance between fun and misery tipped toward fun. We sipped our beer and reverted back to our junior high, high school, and college days, picking on each other unmercifully, reliving previous camping disasters, high-school summer jobs, cross-country motorcycle journeys, and sketchy, long-forgotten girlfriends.

After four years on the island, and less and less contact with my childhood friends, the night reconnected me to my suburban New Jersey past. Rob was reminded that he'd missed a crucial foul shot in a varsity basketball game seventeen years before. George, an undersized halfback and rugby player, was already moving slower with a sore back and funky knees. Four of us were now married; three with children. We were settled into our adult lives, our adult responsibilities.

Momentarily, I worried about my island patients. My mind drifted to the hospital where I'd signed out four islanders to Dr. Phil Slocum.

Had I given him a full report? Would they still be there Monday morning? I felt my shoulders hunch and my neck tighten. I was off call, but my practice always hovered close by.

With a long stick, Rudy poked a boulder out of the fire and rolled it toward the sweat lodge. The boulder glowed red and sizzled steam as he nudged it along. Pulling the flap aside, he pushed the boulder inside. "Boys! Grab a stick! It's SWEAT LODGE TIME!" We followed his lead and soon a jumble of boulders glowed and sizzled in the pit. As our eyes adjusted to the darkness, Rudy came into clear view: He was sitting buck-naked on a log with a canteen of water at his side. "Strip down guys; this is going to be AWESOME!"

The inside of the sweat lodge was already warming up. I brushed off a clump of seaweed from my log, and undressed, taking note of exactly where my snow pants lay and sat on my parka. A pool of water collected beneath our feet where the snow was melting. I can safely say that this was the only time I wore three pairs of socks inside my hiking boots and nothing else.

"Let's do it Rude," I said. "My butt is freezing."

"Okay guys, SHOWTIME!" With that, Rudy emptied his canteen onto the glowing rocks. Steam billowed upwards. Then the rocks exploded like rifle shots. Shards of granite flew everywhere in the darkness. My shins felt like they were on fire. We burst out of the sweat lodge like rats from a sinking ship. I slipped on a rock and fell heavily on my side. The sweat lodge collapsed in a heap. The plastic melted. Toxic steam rose into the sky.

Frantically we pawed through the plastic and driftwood and smoke searching for our clothes in the darkness. I fished out my pants. George found my parka. Rob found George's parka. We dressed more quickly than humanly possible. Remarkably, there were no serious injuries. I fished a flashlight out of my pocket and shone it around. Tux was already dressed. Rudy seemed intent on forcing two legs into one leg of his insulated underwear. My shins were peppered with pockmarks and blood, but nothing looked worthy of stitches. We were okay. We stoked up the bon fire and tried in vain to regain a sense of warmth. Rudy suggested we drink more beer but by now no one was listening to Mr. Sweat Lodge.

As we trudged back to our tents atop Battery Steele, we withdrew into our own private misery. I wormed my way into my sleeping bag and drifted off. Hours later, I awoke, shivering uncontrollably. My mustache was frozen. Tux was humming away in his sleep, but a rime of frost glazed his forehead. He looked annoyingly comfortable. I didn't even want to know how many socks he was wearing. I looked at my watch. It was 9:30. Only nine more hours before sunrise . . .

Morning saved us. I unzipped the fly and poked my head outside the tent and was surprised to see that the other two tents were gone. The ocean was flat to the horizon. Above the sea smoke, a pale, heatless sun rose. I stood outside, stamping my feet and running in place. If it wasn't below zero, it was close. Tux emerged and looked every bit as miserable as I did. We stuffed our gear into our backpacks and walked down to where the truck was parked. On the gun battery cement floor, out of last night's wind, we found George and Rudy folding up their tent. Bruce was gone. Rob explained that Bruce had bailed, crossing the island in the middle of the night, to sleep at my house. Bruce, never one to be swayed by the herd, had reached a point of utter misery and bailed. Smart man.

The truck engine barely turned over, caught, and roared. I flipped on the heater. In a few minutes, I could feel my toes painfully come back to life. We parked in front of the Cockeyed Gull and limped in for breakfast. I looked at my crew. Our faces were smudged with smoke and soot. Each of us wore two knit caps. Like outlaws, our scarves were wrapped around our faces. We settled into our seats and ordered coffee and tea and eggs and muffins and sausage and bacon and pancakes and hot syrup. Richard Erico, a man who knew most everything about Peaks Island, leaned over from an adjacent table and asked, "Dr. Radis, I thought that was you up there on Battery Steele when I drove by this morning. You boys had a hard night?"

Two dozen ears perked up. News on an island travels fast.

By the time, my Cranford friends boarded the Sunday noon ferry for Portland, we were sufficiently thawed out to pronounce the camping trip a resounding success. It felt good to live on the edge, even if it lasted less than 24 hours and our camp site was only a mile from the house. Later that night, I sat inside the sauna Sandi's dad and I had built several years ago. As the electric coils heated the river stones, I hesitated for a moment before emptying the ladle over the stones. The steam rose, curled around, and slapped me in the back of the head. I exhaled and relaxed. It was good medicine.

10

Lois Herndon was morose. Although she was now down to 30 mg of daily prednisone, her face was increasingly round and pudgy and over her upper back, a fat pad, or buffalo hump was clearly present. Lois worked her magic to minimize the changes; she was dressed today in a loose, flowing, floral dress, but complained that "Good god, I look like an overweight hag on a week-long bender."

The bone density I'd ordered demonstrated osteoporosis, and I prescribed estrogen to combat the effects of prednisone on further bone loss. A recent fasting blood sugar was elevated due to prednisone, and Lois was adjusting her diet to avoid diabetic medication. Her tremor? Prednisone. Insomnia? Prednisone. Easy bruising, mood changes, weakness? Prednisone.

Last Tuesday, I reviewed Lois's case at the weekly rheumatology division meeting at Maine Medical Center. As a non-rheumatologist, I found the group welcoming and non-judgmental. The group listened politely but ultimately recommended no change in my treatment plan. They shared their own frustrations with prednisone, particularly when prolonged high-dose treatment was necessary. The oldest physician, Paulding Phelps, recalled that, "until prednisone was developed, your patient's temporal arteritis was a common cause of blindness. The disease was essentially, untreatable."

"Bitch in a bottle," another rheumatologist countered.

"Yes, it's a dirty drug." Dr. Phelps looked at his fellow rheumatologist coolly, before adding, "If you can taper the drug over the next year without her disease flaring, the side-effects will slowly resolve. Most patients need at least twelve to eighteen months of prednisone. Good luck."

The meeting confirmed my sense that Lois was probably doing as well as could be expected. I'd already tried to taper her prednisone more aggressively. When she developed a gnawing, pulsating ache in her forehead, and her erythrocyte sedimentation rate (ESR) skyrocketed, I knew that a slow taper was the only way to go. Hopefully, her repeat ESR would be in the normal range, and I could decrease her prednisone dose slightly.

Marcia Quinby dropped by with a painful elbow. The elbow was exquisitely tender over the outside boney prominence and the diagnosis was straight-forward: lateral epicondylitis, or "tennis elbow." I recommended icing, a Velcro stretch band applied around the forearm, and ibuprofen. If that didn't lead to resolution, I told her, I'd arrange for a course of physical therapy in Portland.

Marcia and David's island business had grown steadily. The puncture wound I'd treated David for healed without complications. Their marriage was a true partnership; David dived year-round collecting specimens while Marcia did the books and packed and mailed the formaldehyde preserved starfish and sea urchins to a scientific supply company. Because their business was in a barn in a residential neighborhood, they were concerned their neighbors would complain about the odor and might pressure the city to shut down their business.

It was not so far-fetched. Late last summer, a local builder broke ground on a 4,000 square foot "starter castle" on the back shore. If the owner were a neighbor of the Quinbys, I doubted she'd be too happy about the formaldehyde. Change was coming to Peaks Island. Each year, more and more cottages were winterized and enlarged; a few were torn down completely. Sandi told me that a new couple on the island recently built a garage, nearly doubling the size of their home up Elizabeth Street. "A garage!" Sandi shook her head in wonder.

I looked on the schedule; Sister Mia was due in after her recent carotid artery surgery. The day after I saw her in the office with her transient ischemic attack, the vascular surgeon convinced her to be hospitalized after reviewing the ultrasound of her carotid artery. At surgery, he was able to "shell out" the plaque narrowing the lumen of the artery, and her recovery was uneventful.

Stepping on the scale, Sister Mia was in good spirits. Between the steroid injection and her new diet, the osteoarthritis in her knee was less painful, and her blood pressure was, if not ideal, at least in the general neighborhood of good. At the end of the office visit, she held my hand in hers and blessed me, Sandi, Kate, and Molly, the Peaks Island community, the surgeon, and the Pope. I didn't confess to her that I had her bag of candy on my desk and was slowly working through the Snickers bars and Milky Ways.

A construction worker I'd recently seen on the island caught my eye as he plopped down in a chair in the waiting room. From my desk, I watched him cross one long leg over the other, and then, restlessly place both feet on the carpet and lean forward with both elbows on his thighs. A few minutes later, inside the exam room, he described a recent flare of back pain so severe a local emergency room physician prescribed several dozen MS Contin (a form of time-released morphine), to treat the pain. "They told me to see you for a refill. The pills worked, but I need a few more, maybe another week's worth, before switching back to Darvocet, my usual pain medicine."

I assessed his reflexes in the lower extremities and strength. I asked him to walk on his heels and then on his toes. Except for "excruciating" pain to palpation in the lower spine, his examination was entirely normal. "The pain," he continued, "was a 10 in the emergency room. Now it's an 8 or 9. If it wasn't for my high pain threshold, I'd be flat on my back."

I had recently attended a lecture on pain management strategies. The lecture was sponsored by Purdue Pharmaceuticals, the maker of MS Contin. Chronic pain has been ignored and under-treated, the lecturer admonished the audience, and physicians should think of pain as the fifth vital sign along with blood pressure, temperature, and heart and respiratory rate. The suggestion made me wince; the traditional vital signs are objective measurements of body function. They are based on physiology and are reproducible. Pain is a symptom, not a sign. Interpreting symptoms is complex and involves judgement and context. Pain, the lecturer suggested, should now be taken at face value. How do we compare pain levels between different patients? It's simple: We give pain a number.

I thought back to the waiting room. The young man's posture and movement did not suggest a disc herniation or other serious back condition. He appeared more like a high-school athlete sitting on the bench hoping for the coach to send him in. Was I obliged to prescribe a narcotic for back pain merely because he assigned his pain an eight or nine?

What's more, MS Contin could be melted down and injected by addicts. Only last month, a young man from Peaks overdosed on a prescription narcotic in the bathroom of the Casco Bay Lines in Portland. I wasn't about to add to the carnage when all I had for evidence was a number.

I am not a complete Luddite when it comes to prescribing narcotics for chronic pain. I had recently prescribed oxycodone to an elderly woman with spinal stenosis who was not a candidate for surgery. Tylenol wasn't working and anti-inflammatories were contra-indicated due to chronic renal insufficiency. When I went over the pros and cons of how one-half tablet of oxycodone twice daily might improve her quality of life, she agreed it was worth a trial.

On a return visit, she was able to ambulate with her walker with less pain. She was constipated, yes, but managed that with an extra daily prune and lots of water. "That pain medicine, you know, the oxy . . . oxy . . . the oxycondom. It protects me from pain."

I surreptitiously opened my pocket calendar and wrote: *oxycondom! Protects me from pain.* Don't let the marketers get hold of that quote.

This "request" by the construction worker was another animal altogether. I decided to be direct; after all, I am not a vending machine where you pay your money and pick out your candy. I closed the young man's chart and looked him in the eye. "I'm not going to prescribe any more MS Contin, but . . . I can perform some gentle soft-tissue manipulation and prescribe a muscle relaxant for your back. I think that will help."

"You mean, you're not going to help me out? What kind of doctor are you?" he said, his voice rising.

"No. I'm not giving you a prescription of MS Contin. If you want to lie back down, I can work on your back . . ."

The young man scrambled up from the table, grabbed his coat, and stormed out. In the waiting room filled with patients, he turned and shouted back, "Dr. Radis is a f—ing quack! I wouldn't trust him with my dog!"

I realized that I was clutching the exam room doorknob like a vise. When I released my hand, I noticed a slight tremor in my right hand. Back inside the exam room, I changed out the paper sheet on the table, and realized that the cabinet above the sink was slightly ajar. Spilled out on the shelf were a handful of diabetic needles and syringes. I am not absolutely sure that any were taken. I opened my pocket calendar and wrote: *Talk with police. Lock cabinets!*

Then I cleared my mind and asked Anne to room the next patient.

One of the most difficult transitions in medicine is to refocus after a traumatic encounter. Today, this was made easier because Sister Marie-Henry was my next patient. She was blissfully unaware of the commotion. For one, she was stone deaf. For another, the curvature of her back from multiple compression fractures angled her head downward, which was fine for reading or praying, but spared her the dramatic exit of my back-pain patient.

Watching her shuffle forward, it was impossible not to ignore the contrast between the young man demanding narcotics for his pain, and Sister Marie-Henry's insistence that Tylenol worked just fine. Her recent x-rays of the spine demonstrated four compression fractures of varying age. On one foot was a brace, around her torso was a corset to firm up the spine. Yet, she met me with a shy, beatific, smile and reported that it was a miracle; she was pain free.

The visit with Sister Marie-Henry lifted me up and reset my day. I regained my focus and was able to assess and problem solve without residual frustration or anger. Over a peanut butter and jelly lunch at my desk, I spent a few extra minutes carefully documenting my rationale for refusing to prescribe MS Contin to the construction worker.

As I leafed through a medical journal, a full-page advertisement caught my eye. It portrayed a physician writing a prescription for a back-pain patient who appeared to be in considerable distress. You knew that the pain must be a high number because the patient was grimacing. The caption read: *Pain, the 5th vital sign.* The advertisement was sponsored by Purdue Frederick for MS Contin. We're in for it now, I thought.

That night I received a frantic call; the police were at a cottage trying to revive a middle-aged woman who had collapsed shortly after dinner. By the time I arrived at the house, officer Mike and big John were already performing CPR on an overweight heavy-set, middle-aged woman on the living room floor. It was a ghoulish scene with the contents of the woman's last meal splattered onto her chest and officer Mike methodically performing chest compressions.

I stood back for a moment and assessed the scene. The woman's face and extremities were an ominous pale blue despite the CPR and oxygen. I squatted next to Mike and felt for a pulse. No pulse. Cardiac arrest? Food blocking the wind pipe? Drug overdose? I asked the police to stop CPR for a moment and listened for heart sounds. Nothing. Mike resumed CPR while I removed the wrapping from an endotracheal tube I kept in a side compartment of my black bag and positioned myself at the woman's head.

"How long has she been down?" I asked officer Mike.

"Maybe 15 minutes. Her husband called us at . . . "

"8:05." Big John glanced at a clipboard as he adjusted the high-flow oxygen. "We arrived at 8:15. He was watching TV as she walked into the living room, said she just dropped. Fireboats on the way."

"Okay, off the chest." I tilted the woman's head slightly backwards and slid the laryngoscope into her mouth. Food and mucus made visualization of the upper trachea difficult. I removed the scope and cleaned out my patient's mouth as best I could while Mike resumed chest compressions. Once again, I inserted the laryngoscope with my left hand and held the endotracheal tube in my right, hoping to visualize my landmarks. There! The fleshy knob of the epiglottis swung into view. I pulled upwards with the laryngoscope and in the same motion slid the endotracheal tube into what I hoped was the upper trachea.

Big John taped the tube in place while Mike continued chest compressions. I listened to both lung fields, hoping that the position of the tube was correct. Good, a steady stream of oxygen was flowing into the lungs; that ruled out an obstruction from a piece of meat. Still no pulse.

Officer Mike glanced over. "Fireboat will be at the dock soon. We should move her."

The three of us placed the woman on a gurney and awkwardly continued chest compressions. As we wheeled her out to the ambulance, the last image I saw was of the living room, her husband in his recliner, slumped over, hands to his face, weeping. A young woman silently passed us on the way in as we transferred his wife to the ambulance, all the while performing CPR. When the fireboat arrived, I hopped onboard. My job was largely done; under the direction of a Maine Med ER physician, the emergency medical technicians on-board continued CPR and inserted an IV. Her care was now out of my hands. A series of medications were injected in hopes of retrieving a pulse. We looked at the monitor; the EKG was flat-line.

As we pulled into the Portland, one of the EMT soberly looked up. "How long has she been down?"

I looked at my watch. "Her husband called at 8:05. It's been fifty minutes." We both knew that further CPR was futile. The Maine Med ER physician gently recommended that we stop. There was an awkward silence before I reluctantly agreed.

On the Portland side, we silently loaded the woman onto an awaiting ambulance, and it slowly pulled away. I went into the nearby ferry terminal bathroom to wash up. I wondered why I couldn't cry. The deceased woman was 48, nearly the same age as my father when he died of a massive heart attack. Growing up, I can't recall crying at my father's funeral. Walking home that night, the tears finally came. After the ferry delivered me back to Peaks, I walked home, alone in my thoughts, passing by the woman's cottage. The light was on, and a dim figure was visible behind the blinds. I knocked on the door

The next morning, I turned on the faucet to brush my teeth and waited. Then I gamely waved the toothbrush beneath the faucet as if this might trigger . . . something. "Sandi, I think the pipes froze."

"Not so loud. Kate and Molly are sleeping. Grab the hairdryer."

In the predawn darkness, the wind rattled the double-hung window above the toilet and slammed against the shingles on the outside wall. I opened the cabinet door beneath the sink and a waft of frigid air flowed against my hand. The insulation in the wall behind the sink must have settled, or the pipe might have been frozen where the heat tape couldn't reach between the first and second floor. The memory of the unsuccessful resuscitation the previous night was momentarily pushed aside. Today was Saturday, a rare day off.

I plugged in the hairdryer and pointed it directly at the plumbing. By then, Sandi was up, balancing Molly on one hip and carrying the space heater in the other. We plugged in the space heater, repeated the process in the downstairs bathroom directly below, and waited. Water expands in a frozen pipe and may crack the copper tubing. We'd been lucky so far; a burst pipe is a winter disaster.

As abruptly as the wind came up, it lay back and the bay settled down as soon as the sun peeked over the hillside above the house. A thin mist wafted across the channel between Peaks and Little Diamond Island. I put a pot of water on the stove and after it came to a rolling boil, poured Sandi a cup for tea, filled Molly's bowl to heat up her breakfast bourra (a Finnish breakfast cereal Sandi was raised on), and half-filled my mug with the remainder for instant coffee. Kate walked blearily into the kitchen, holding her favorite blanket. "It's cold in my room," she said.

"That's why you need to wear socks to bed," Sandi replied.

"Okay."

It was our fourth winter on the island and we still did not have an air-tight house. Not that we hadn't tried. The first summer, before we hired a builder to transform the structure from an un-insulated cottage to a year-round home, I asked Sandi's dad for advice. The former dairy farmer put on a pair of boots and bowed his head when he entered the crawl space where there was a foot of water. He put a level on the uneven floor in the living room. He stuck his measuring tape into a gap in the drywall and said, "This is traditional one by three cottage construction."

"What does that mean?" We asked.

"It means that you have less room for insulation. Does it get very cold out here?"

Sandi and I looked at each other and shrugged. "Maybe."

"You'd be better off tearing the whole thing down and starting over."

"But what do you really think?" I asked my father-in-law. He silently pulled a lighter from his pocket and flicked it on.

During breakfast, the ice jam let loose with a low-pitched rumble. I turned on the hot water upstairs and let it run. For good measure, we kept the space heaters running for another hour. The phone rang. It was Sandi's boss Paul, and he needed help with three other houses with frozen pipes. It was a Saturday and he promised Sandi time and a half. I offered to take the children sledding and feed them lunch. Paul thought they'd be finished by early afternoon. In a few minutes Sandi was in her work clothes and out the door. The temperature outside was up to eight degrees.

After watching Saturday morning cartoons, I bundled up Kate and Molly, packed a thermos of hot chocolate, and threw our sleds into the back of the truck. Stopping at Feeney's Market, I left the girls in the chip aisle to pick out a treat while I grabbed a loaf of bread. A young woman in the produce section pulled me aside and said, "I don't want to bother you, but should I be worried about my elbow?"

Before I could respond, she rolled up her coat sleeve and a moment later I was looking at a fluid filled, egg-sized sack on the posterior aspect of the elbow. I ran my hand over the outlines of the sac, decided it probably wasn't infected, and said, "It looks like an inflamed bursa. Icing it and taking ibuprofen should shrink it down, but if that doesn't work, you should stop by the clinic and I can drain it."

At the check-out counter there was another delay; this time to update the husband of a woman who had been admitted to my service at the hospital with abdominal pain and underwent a cholecystectomy (gall bladder surgery) several days before. I explained that my coverage was taking care of his wife this weekend but that if all went well, she'd be home Monday or Tuesday. Back inside the truck I cracked open my pocket calendar and wrote: *Avoid store if in a hurry.*

On our way to Tolman Heights, the best sledding hill on the island, I flipped the heater on high and Kate and Molly opened up their bag of Doritos. I wished Sandi was with us. Between my long hours and Sandi's part-time work and managing the children, we have precious little time together. At times, it seemed like life was one big hand-off. Counseling had helped last year and we had a better understanding of each other's needs and expectations, but understanding only goes so far. We needed a date; maybe tonight.

Turning the corner to the back shore, I pointed out sea smoke to the girls and explained that on the coldest winter mornings when the bay was still, the mist could play tricks and create optical illusions. As if to prove my point, Kate pointed to Outer Green and Junk of Pork islands on the horizon. "Look daddy. They're floating!" And it was true; the two distant islands seemed to float on a bed of sea smoke, suspended above the water. Molly asked, "Daddy, what is oppy dusion?"

We grabbed our sleds from the back of the truck, but before I could react, Molly shouted, "Look at me!" and slid down a slab of ice onto the beach, tumbling into a rocky bed of seaweed. For a two-year-old in a bulky snowsuit she moved like an unpredictable teenager. I'd have to watch that. Before I could react, Kate barreled off the same slab, narrowly missing her sister, and thudded to a stop against a refrigerator-sized boulder.

I shook my head; five minutes into sledding, and the girl's snowsuits were already soaked. No matter; fun was in the air. For the next several hours, we rocketed down from Tolman Heights (at 87 feet, one of the highest points on the island) on an unplowed road toward Spar Cove. Other families joined in. A snowman was constructed. I held Molly in my sled while Kate rode her plastic sled standing up, which worked well until she hit a bump and the sled went one way and Kate another. Nice try. Molly wiggled out of my arms and raced over to her sister. The two sisters lay giggling, face down in the snow. A few minutes later, Molly collapsed in my arms and cried for no apparent reason. It was time to go.

On our way back to the house, Rick Crowley waved me over and rolled down the window of his truck. "Scallop season's nearly done, maybe another day or two before we reach the quota and the state closes us down.

Scalloping! This was the invitation I'd been hoping for, but, I remembered, probably not today. "Got the kids. Sandi's working with Paul, thawing out frozen pipes."

"If you make it, you make it. Meet me at the army pier in an hour Wear something you can get soaked in." Rick pulled a can of beer out from between his legs and took a long, slow draw before putting the truck in gear. Back home, I fed Kate and Molly and put them both down for naps. I glanced out the upstairs window and saw Sandi coming down the walkway. Snow was drifting down and sticking to the withered tassels of last summer's goldenrod. After a quick lunch, Sandi joined the kids for a nap, but not before encouraging me to join Rick for a few hours. "Remember? The ladies' ballgown party is tonight at the Landing!"

Ah, yes, the ballgown party. There went our date. The event is another example of Sandi's appealing eccentricity. With her friend, Rose-Anne, she founded the Peaks Island ballgown celebration several years ago to break the winter doldrums. It began as a celebration of Sandi's birthday month: January. A dozen or so women came to our house wearing tiaras and costume jewelry and outlandish puffy dresses. One young mother wore her dress backwards. Cake, wine, and chocolate were consumed.

The next year, Sandi decided, why not open the event up to the island? Robin Clark, owner of the Landing, a seasonal restaurant, offered free space. Sandi and Rose-Anne drafted basic ground rules: Ladies only. There would be a cash bar. The ballgown must be purchased from Goodwill or the Salvation Army for less than $10 or be an old bridesmaid dress. Zipping up the back (or front) was optional. Duct tape was recommended as the preferred fastener. The party would end at 9:00 p.m.

The first year sixty women showed up; the next more than a hundred. Tinsel and balloons and crepe paper are suspended by thumb tacks from the ceiling and walls. Two speakers on top of the bar blare Sandi's favorite mix of Broadway show tunes and rock'n'roll. The only man in sight would be a life-sized cardboard cutout of Fabio. Most conversations, I've been told, focus on telling each other how spectacular they look. The past year, a grandmother in her 70s, her daughter, and teenage granddaughter made the scene. For a few hours every year, the dreariness and darkness of winter, the responsibilities of work and children, are pushed aside. Everyone is a princess.

When Sandi flicks the lights at 8:45, nearly everyone is ready to call it a night. Those who want to continue the party walk unsteadily up the hill to the Legion Hall.

I changed into insulated underwear and jeans and a gray sweatshirt and boarded *E Cosi* as it pushed off into the channel between Peaks and House Island. Heavy snow covered the deck. Rick handed me a shovel. His boat, *E Cosi* (Italian for: and so?), was a fifty-foot dragger built in 1960 in Montauk, at the eastern tip of Long Island. Rick did nearly all of the engine repairs. Without the skills of a tinkerer to keep overhead down, Rick admitted he'd never make a profit. The margin in fishing, as in farming, is slim, and to be successful, you can't hire out every dinky repair if you're going to make a go of it.

Nancy, Rick's wife, waved and invited me inside her workstation. The unpainted, rough-cut plywood shack sported a flat roof with a small water-side window. It's there, out of the wind, where she'd work up our catch. Nancy wore rubber boots, a loose wool cap, a waterproof smock, and a yellow slicker over a sweater. Leaning into the shack to shake her hand, I noticed that her blue eyes unexpectedly glistened; each lash, both upper and lower, was darkened and separated. When she removed her gloves, I noticed that her nails were manicured.

She reminded me of a calendar that I thought someone should create. I even had a name for it: *Working Women of Casco Bay.* There are a lot of tough, capable women on these islands. Sandi, of course, would be Miss January—her birthday month—discreet, and carrying two wrenches. Bev Johnson, another woman plumber from neighboring Long Island, would be a nice addition. So would Lisa at the coffee shop, and Lisa the landscaper. Yohanna Von Tiling, a retired teacher from Cliff Island, and well into her 80s, aka the *Queen of Casco Bay,* was an absolute must.

I had to hold that thought. We were about to begin. Rick eased the engine into neutral. "Ready for some work?" He zipped up his light jacket and gingerly picked his way to the stern through a jumble of cables.

The key to successful scalloping begins with a ten-foot, 300-pound metal bar that drags across the bottom on rollers. Flowing out from the back of the bar are interconnected rings forming the outlines of a net. To keep the mouth of the net open, a string of softball-sized floats plays out on the upper edge of the net. A thick wire harness is fastened to the ends of the bar, and at the mid-point of this rig, a stainless steel eye-hook connects the bar to a cable running over a metal cradle to a hydraulic drum inside the pilot house.

Dragging for scallops takes into account two remarkable abilities scallops possess that clams and oysters do not: Scallops have eyes, and they can swim, or scoot, short distances. As many as one hundred individual cobalt blue eyes line the open carapace of a bay scallop. When a shadow of a starfish or other predator is perceived, scallops flap their shells and propel themselves out of harm's way. Scallop draggers take advantage of this; most scallops fly upwards, away from the approaching bar, into the open trailing net. But there are the fortunate few who flutter off to either side and resettle to the bottom, out of harm's way. The process is not easy on the seabed.

Back inside the wheelhouse, Rick flipped on the hydraulic winch and guided the gear over the stern into the water. The cable played out a good fifty yards behind the boat. Then he returned to his captain's seat and maintained his course parallel to House Island by following an electronic plot map for our first tow.

Watching Rick from the side, I was struck by his eyes, the same blue as Nancy's. Constantly in motion, they shifted back and forth between the chart and the smudged windshield. I'm not sure why he even bothered to look out when he said, "You don't need no damn windows to know where you're going," which was disconcerting in the near white-out conditions. He added, "There are three things that bring bad luck to a boat: umbrellas, suitcases, and bananas." I thought to myself, isn't there a woman in there somewhere?

Momentarily, we had nothing to do. Snow fell like a heavy blanket onto the slate gray surface of the water. A distant buoy clanged. A flock of seagulls hovered over the boat, squawking and screeching for handouts. Nancy came into the wheelhouse and placed a hand on Rick's shoulder. She told me she was a French Lit major in college and went to work for an Italian airline after graduation. She'd been married nearly forty years before divorcing and moving to Peaks Island. There, she met Rick, who was laying floor at her house. They hit it off and were married several years ago. Scalloping? She says the season is her favorite time of year.

"Watch her work a scallop knife," Rick said. "She's the best in the business. Top-end restaurants don't want a nicked-up ragged scallop. They want a scallop looking like it's been plucked from a tree and they'll pay a premium for it."

Nancy returned to her plywood "apartment" and readied her workstation for the first tow. Rick said she was the best thing that ever happened to him. It wasn't his first marriage, and he offered that he was able to shake a vague "drug problem," a few years before meeting her. During that time, he lost his lobster license and deep-water scalloping federal license because he didn't pay to keep them updated. He came from a big family on Peaks, five siblings and five adopted siblings, and had spent his entire adult life on the water. Thankfully, he'd kept his inshore scallop license.

"Ready for some fun?" Rick stood over the hydraulic cable spool, pushed a red control lever forward, and engaged the spool. With another lever, he set the drum in motion. I noticed a loose edge of his sweatshirt dangling over the spinning drum. Without looking up, Rick tucked in the sweatshirt and said, "This is Maine's most dangerous fishery."

I noted the cables on the deck and the spinning drum, and thought, *watch your step, there are a lot of nooks and crannies on this boat where something very bad can go wrong.*

The drum slowly filled with cable and a block of churning white water signaled that the drag was near the surface. The rig emerged from the water, suspended over the deck. Rick picked his way aft and maneuvered the bar here and there much like a worker on the ground might move a massive cement water main held by a crane. He meticulously picked out the detritus snared on the outside of the net, including several crushed ghost lobster traps (traps no longer connected to the surface), a shovel, several tires, and a blue plastic barrel. Dissatisfied with what he could reach from the deck, he climbed the circular rings to reach a snarl of rope and cut it out with a long knife.

Then Rick stepped back a few feet and signaled to Nancy in the pilot house to release the tow. Rockweed and sponge, sea anemone, starfish, sea squirts, rock and green crab, sea cucumber, empty oyster shells and razor clams tumbled onto the open deck. I was disappointed. I expected a mother lode of scallops. An eel slithered underfoot and wiggled out the scupper. Rick noticed a large flounder flapping beneath a clump of seaweed and quickly tossed it into a plastic tote. Two lobster were tossed overboard; they're illegal to keep unless caught in a traditional trap.

Nancy handed me a four-inch metal ring as we bent down on our hands and knees and went through the catch, searching for our quarry. "If a scallop passes through the ring, it's undersized," she explained. "Throw it overboard with everything else. If it's legal, tap it with the ring. A mudder, a dead scallop, sounds different than a live scallop. You'll learn." I didn't have long to wait. When I pulled back on a clump of rockweed, four scallops, two of them legal-sized, appeared like four-leaf clovers. Nancy handed me a plastic basket and I tossed the scallops inside. At the end of the first tow, my basket contained twenty-seven scallops. The rest of the catch, hundreds of pounds of the living and the dead, was pushed overboard through the scuppers. Despite the plastic gloves and kneepads, it was slippery, bone-chilling work.

Rick re-attached a grab hook to the harness while Nancy combined our two baskets into one and lugged the scallops to her work shack. The net slowly rose overhead and dipped over the stern. Rick played out the cable.

I ducked my head into Nancy's workstation as she deftly inserted the shucking blade into a shell at the hinge, twisted the knife, and cut the adductor muscle from its attachment. With a scooping twisting motion, she separated the "guts" of the scallop . . . liver, intestine, gills, and heart, and flicked the gob overboard. Then, with a more measured, deft cut, she separated the scallop meat from the remaining shell and dropped the ivory plug into a clean bucket of salt water.

She talked as she worked, flashing her knife for emphasis. She poked a small fish with her finger where it nestled inside an open scallop before flinging it over the side. "It's a hake; it's always a hake." A herring gull, hovering just outside Nancy's window, barely missed the morsel. She handed me an irregular piece of off-white, gravel. "It's a pearl. Not worth much, but I think they're beautiful."

I returned to the wheelhouse and held my hands over the heat vent. Rick handed me a pair of dry, rubber gloves. "Only twelve more tows and we'll call it a day."

"So, what's the strangest thing you ever pulled up in the net?" I asked.

"Every once in a while, one of the boats will drag up live ordnance from World War II. What are you going to do? Throw it back? Leave it on the deck all day? The whole deal is a pain in the butt. I'd rather pull up something useful, like coal. A coal barge must have sunk off Cushing Island years ago. We harvest it every winter just off the point. Burns great in our wood stove. But that's not the strangest thing we've seen out here. Last fall we had a brown pelican. It followed the boat for the better part of a week."

Nancy chimed in from her workstation, "I think it must have gotten caught up in a hurricane down south and blown north. The other boats saw it too. Strangest sight I've ever seen. It ate every scrap we threw overboard; the gulls got nothing."

I wasn't absolutely certain, but between the coal and the pelican story, my skepticism meter was flatlining. "How much do you get for your scallops?" I asked, changing the topic.

Nancy rattled off the numbers. "If we sell them to a dealer, we get about $14 a pound for U-8, meaning eight scallops to a pound; U-10, a bit less. People love the bigger scallops but there's nothing tastier than a bay scallop. Fresh off the boat, we sell some of the catch to islanders to avoid the middleman and pick up a few extra bucks."

"What about frozen scallops?"

"If you do it right, frozen scallops keep just fine," Rick said as he left his seat and engaged the hydraulics to pull in the next tow. "On days we don't sell out, we flash freeze the rest and sell it out of the house. What you want to see in a freshly caught scallop is an ivory or cream color. A white scallop looks good, but it's probably been injected with water or chemicals to plump it up."

Twenty minutes later, the drag balanced over the stern and another haul spilled out on the deck. This time, Nancy and I collected thirty-eight legal-sized scallops. The snow turned to a light sleet and the deck became dangerously slick. Nancy picked up her basket of scallops as if it were a load of laundry and disappeared into her shack. She stuck her head out the door and invited me in to watch her work. "People are always looking for a way to cheat. Meat from a skate that is punched out with a cookie cutter can look like a scallop, but if you look carefully, the fibers aren't running up and down like the meat of a scallop."

As the afternoon wore on, I did my best to hide my absolute misery. In between tows I stood in the pilot house with Captain Rick. Pieces of insulated wire, rusted bolts, and a variety of wrenches and pliers littered the console. Once Rick thought he heard a strange noise coming from the engine room and leaving me at the wheel, lifted up the hatch amidships and descended a metal ladder with a flashlight. A moment later, he was back on deck. "False alarm."

On our fourteenth tow, Captain Rick declared it was time to call it a day. Nancy and I scavenged thirty scallops for a grand total of four hundred and ninety, translating to roughly fifty pounds of scallop meat. Nancy gave the scallops a final wash and, satisfied, stowed the bucket beneath her workstation. I noticed on the wall, at eye level, a color photo of Nancy in work gear. . . with a pelican gliding lazily by her window.

Rick dropped me off at the public safety float and pointed *E Cosi* toward its mooring. "Banker's hours," Rick said, as he pushed off. He was grinning broadly. It had been a successful day. I was neither an umbrella, suitcase, nor banana. I'd worked hard, not complained, and quietly done my job.

At home, Sandi was resplendent in her gown. Then she tried on several more before leaving for the ball. I was exhausted, but it was a good exhaustion. I love medicine, but it was good to get out on the water for an afternoon of restorative grunt work. We would have our date soon enough.

12

Yesterday I spotted the season's first iridescent blue and gold crocus poking through a patch of snow on my walk to clinic. Today, there were six, in a small clump, with the flowers leaning toward the sun. Within a few days, a week at most, the petals would wilt and drop and, if the warming trend held, other spring flowers would pick up the beat: daffodils, coltsfoot, blue violet, wild geranium.

But my favorite, the most difficult to spy before the ethereal half-inch white flowers disappeared was goldthread, a ground-hugging resident of the island's spruce understory. And it's not the flower alone that delights me; just beneath the surface is a thread-like, orange rhizome, the source of a bitter herbal remedy for cold sores and intestinal parasites. Though Peaks has been settled and farmed for hundreds of years, with the interior meadows reclaimed by red spruce and white pine, goldthread was back. More likely, it never left.

I arrived at the health center a few minutes early. Setting my green satchel and daypack on my desk, I thumbed through the charts Anne had pulled for the morning's clinic. Today, not necessarily by design, was mental-illness day at the health center. Some of my long-term patients had improved, either with medications alone or in combination with counseling. Others floundered under the influence of co-existing alcohol or drug addictions. They were self-medicating their post-traumatic stress disorder or psychosis or major depression in the most destructive way possible; entangling loved ones in a web of anger, neglect, and sometimes, emotional and physical abuse.

There were those on the day's schedule who would deny they had mental illness. These patients saw me for their diabetes or irritable bowel syndrome or headaches or heart disease, but didn't recognize how their mental health affected their physical health. Or, if they did, their emotional baggage, their burden of sadness, was so heavy they lacked the tools to make major lifestyle changes.

It was these particular visits that exhausted and frustrated me because, all too often, I felt like a garage mechanic on speed dial: here's my body, I'll come back in a half hour and take the pill you recommend. These were the "Yes, but. . ." visits. If I recommended a therapist. the patient replied, "Yes, but. . ." I tried that once and it didn't work. If I recommended walking to reduce weight and help with anxiety, the patient would agree, "Yes, but. . . I'm too exhausted, or my knees hurt, or I don't have time."

In these patients, I prescribed a boatload of medications with only minor benefit. Or, as the Chinese proverb says: "If we don't change the direction we're headed, we'll end up where we are going."

My first patient was an overweight woman with diabetes and unacknowledged alcoholism. I knew this because most everyone on Peaks Island was aware of her heavy drinking. She lived alone and staggered into the library twice a week. On the way home, laden with books, she bought a quart of Johnnie Walker and a quart of gin at Feeney's Market.

This was her fourth visit with me and she hid her sadness behind a quick wit. A few months ago, on the new patient questionnaire, under alcohol use, she'd written: "Whatever." Under family history, she kidded, "We have a huge family that are related." Today was the first time I was seeing her in the office after she'd admitted to being deeply depressed, didn't want to see a counselor, but was willing to start fluoxetine (Prozac). I had a vague sense that she was a suicide risk even if she wouldn't admit whether the thought had ever crossed her mind. It's why I'd picked Prozac as an anti-depressant; the drug is nearly impossible to overdose on. On the other hand, combining it with alcohol could be problematic.

"Did the Prozac help?" I asked.

"Well, to tell you the truth, I'm not really sure. Maybe. I'm borderline upright." She stared out the window following the flight of a crow as it harassed a blue jay on the oak Sister Marie Henry had backed into the past week.

"Any side effects? Have you been able to get out and walk?"

"No, I forgot about that. It's all I can do to drag myself up and down the stairs. I feel like I have rocks in my pockets and I'm walking through a river of molasses."

She was an expert at pivoting the conversation and after fifteen minutes of trying to initiate a meaningful conversation it was clear she didn't want to talk about why she was depressed. Mostly, it seemed, she just wanted a pill to take the edge off. She had a dog, Lilly, and we chatted about that. At the end of the visit, I walked her out to the checkout counter and Anne made a follow-up appointment in two weeks.

Back at my desk, as I closed her chart and placed it on the shelf, a letter drifted onto the floor. It was from an out-of-state psychiatrist and written more than twenty-five years before, when the patient lived in the Midwest. The letter described the trauma she and her three sisters had experienced when their mother confronted a burglar and the intruder shot the mother dead in front of the children. The man was eventually caught and sentenced to life in prison.

In an instant, my entire view of my patient was turned on its head. I re-read the letter. How does one survive a trauma of that magnitude? How does one have the will to go on? Do I share the letter with her? Instead, I decided to share my concerns with Sandi. As a former family counselor, she might have some suggestions on how to discuss the letter with the woman or connect her with someone far more capable of treating her than I.

Shortly after we moved to Peaks Island, Sandi briefly considered opening a part-time family therapy practice on Peaks before she left her position at Community Counseling in Portland for plumbing and electrical work. Ultimately, the thought of seeing her clients at the post office, at Feeney's Market, and on the ferry was too close for comfort. In Feeney's Market, she wanted to concentrate on the grocery list, not on the problems of the young woman shopping in aisle two. And there was a practical side of her decision. Now that I was avoiding Feeney's, someone in our family had to pick up groceries.

I told myself that my mental illness case load was no different from other rural physician's. But that wasn't necessarily true. Between the ferry, walking, busing, or driving to an appointment, and timing the return ferry home, it was often a four- to five-hour round-trip for my patients to see a counselor. When I described to a psychiatry friend the challenges I faced on the islands, he concluded that the more severe the psychiatric disorder, the less likely a patient would connect with a mental health professional in Portland. "Congratulations, you are their de facto mental health worker." And that had been my experience. For now, prior to each visit, I tried to clear my head, rev up my empathy cap, and look for opportunities to make each patient's journey a little easier.

Dan was my next patient. At five-foot-nine, 120 pounds, he was chronically thirty pounds underweight. Although he had always suffered from "nervousness," his life changed dramatically when he rear-ended a truck in Portland while nibbling on a sausage sandwich. His head had struck the windshield and he'd fractured several ribs on the steering wheel, but it was the sausage sandwich that left the most indelible scars. When rescuers found Dan, he was frantically clawing at his partially blocked airway. The sausage was successfully removed, but the emotional trauma left him a psychological cripple.

For five years he had subsisted on liquid nutritional supplements despite there being no physical reason why he couldn't chew and swallow solid food. His wife, a pleasant, ruddy-cheeked woman, brought him to appointments and sat in on our visits. She was respectful and optimistic, steadfast in the believe that we were only one intervention away from restoring her husband to a more normal life. But nothing seemed to work. Last year, Dan was briefly admitted to the hospital when his weight dipped under 115 pounds and he suffered a grand mal seizure from an electrolyte imbalance. Psychiatry and neurology consulted and prescribed a slew of medications—crushed and suspended in a milkshake—but there was no progress toward solving the underlying swallowing disorder.

As I leafed through the chart, I reviewed the barium swallow study of the esophagus and the MRI scan of his head from that admission. Both were normal. At least we knew there wasn't an unusual stroke syndrome or esophageal disorder affecting his swallowing mechanism.

I had an idea. "Why don't we begin with a tiny crumb?" I suggested. Dan and his wife considered this and agreed that it wouldn't hurt to try. I broke off a small piece of blueberry muffin his wife had bought at Lisa's coffee shop. Then I dropped the fragment onto Dan's outstretched palm and asked, "Why don't you give it a try?"

Dan picked up the crumb off her palm with his free hand. He eyed the morsel skeptically, and held it up to the light and turned it this way and that, as if he were solving a puzzle. Then he placed it in his mouth.

His wife glowed, "Now we're getting somewhere!"

Then Dan swallowed, or rather, attempted to swallow. He gagged. His chin jutted forward as he made bobbing motions with his head. His eyes flared and blinked. After a few seconds, he retrieved the wet fragment and carefully divided it in half and returned it to his mouth. Tears rolled down his cheeks. More head bobbing and gagging. He spit the blueberry muffin crumb into the sink.

"I'm so proud of you for trying," I said, and patted him on the shoulder. "You'll do it. Maybe trying it in front of us isn't the way to go. Pick out something you really like. What kind of food do you miss? Is there a food you can try at home?"

"I like Pop Tarts."

"Well then, a tiny piece of Pop Tart might be the ticket," I said, trying to sound upbeat. "Maybe you can experiment. Practice chewing. When you're ready, give it a try."

"I'd be scared to try it by myself," he answered. "What if I choked again and no one was around?" His wife patted him on a thigh. The visit was, essentially, over.

"Is it okay if I draw some blood?" I said softly. "I want to make sure your electrolytes and medication levels are normal." His eyes emptied out as he extended an arm. His failure to manage even a single crumb signaled the depth and complexity of his illness.

A young woman in her late twenties was next. For the past year I had seen her with progressive fatigue, body aches, and joint pain. Her primary diagnosis was depression; her secondary diagnosis was fibromyalgia, a painful musculoskeletal pain syndrome. After each visit, I dutifully jotted a few words of hers in her chart summarizing her plight: "I'm getting worse," or "The pain is excruciating," or "I don't know how much more I can take." Medication trials had been disappointing. Even simple measures such as stretching and yoga had triggered flares of pain. Today, she wanted to let me know she was moving to Arizona to see a special friend. She looked radiant, comfortable, relaxed. I suspected she was in love. "I'm cured," she laughed as she turned to go. "I don't know what I would have done without you."

There are patients for whom I suspect I make a difference. An elderly man down the way from our house was next. He saw me monthly for a blood pressure check, but we focused primarily on strategies to help him deal with his wife Grace's progressive dementia. Through our office visits I knew that they'd had a sweet, more-than-45-year marriage. When he said, "I miss her," I understood; he was no longer her friend and partner, he had become her full-time caregiver. Medications had helped Grace a bit, but each month brought a new challenge. I'd connected the husband with a home health aide for respite care. The aide did some light cleaning for the couple and sat with Grace while she watched television, enabling the husband to slip outside for a daily walk with a friend.

Walking was also a saving grace for Grace, who, each morning, regardless of the weather, dutifully plodded the mile to Feeney's Market to buy a pack of cigarettes and purchase a newspaper she never read. On the way home, she might sing or whistle an old-time tune. Getting lost on an island could happen, but so far, there were enough familiar faces to point Grace in the right direction.

At the conclusion of the visit, I suggest that the husband play old records at home. "Grace might sing along—Alzheimer's patients often recall the words and melodies to songs long after they've forgotten most everything else."

"It's worth a try," the husband replied. "Before we met, she was a camp counselor. Believe me, she knew every verse of every camp song ever written."

We stood and I shook his hand; I do a lot of shaking hands or patting shoulders in my practice. Ignoring my hand, he moved in for a bear hug and, releasing me, quickly walked out to the front desk to settle his bill. The next morning, I saw him walking with his wife past our house. The two were singing softly and holding hands. Of course, with Alzheimer's, it wouldn't last, but at that moment a melody connected them in a lovely way.

The police called. An elderly woman up one of the interior dirt roads needed to be transferred to Portland with shortness of breath and fever but was not cooperating. She called the emergency number but now refused to leave her home. They told me her name and I understood why they were calling; she had schizophrenia and might have discontinued her medications. Anne whispered to me that my last two patients of the morning had canceled. I had about an hour before the next ferry. I told the police I'd be right over.

As I filled a compartment of my green satchel with blood and urine specimens to drop off at the hospital, I mulled over the morning and decided it went as well as can be expected. I biked up the dirt road toward the center of the island and reviewed what little I knew about the woman. I'd seen Ruth briefly two years before for a visit soon after her discharge from P-6, a locked mental health ward at Maine Medical Center. At the time she was prescribed Thorazine, a powerful antipsychotic. I have no idea if she followed through with a psychiatrist in town, but I'm certain I never saw her again at the health center.

Officers Mike and John met me outside the cottage. Mike, in particular, was on edge. "She looks terrible, high fever, respiratory rate thirty per minute. The fireboat is sitting on the public safety float, waiting. She definitely needs to come to town but won't get on the stretcher."

"I see," I said, thinking, *and you think I can convince her?* I took another look at the cottage. Several grey asbestos shingles lay scattered on the ground. Ripped tar paper and plywood peeked through the missing shingles. The chimney was tilted and moss grew on the sagging roof. A foot path lined with striking cream-colored daffodils led to the front door. Okay, here goes. I knocked lightly and announced that I was Dr. Radis.

A gravelly voice barked from inside, "Go away. I have pneumonia. You might catch a cold."

"That's very considerate of you, Ruth," I answered. "Thank you. May I come in and visit?" There was a brief silence. Then a pair of puffy eyes peered through a crack in the shade. Fortunately, Mike and

John had, by now, moved the ambulance, and were nowhere in sight. I smiled and waved politely before reaching into my green satchel and placed my stethoscope around my neck.

The door creaked open, followed by the sound of shoes scurrying away. I cautiously stepped inside. My patient was in bed, a white sheet pulled up over her head like a corpse. Empty packing boxes, candy wrappers, shopping bags, magazines, and a large fishing net lay on the floor. On the bed stand was a loaf of bread and an empty opaque, orange pill container labeled: Thorazine. The expiration date was six -months ago. I recognized the prescriber's name as a Portland psychiatrist.

"Hello. Thanks for letting me in."

There was no answer from the corpse. I counted the rhythmic up and down movement of the sheet. At thirty, her respiratory rate was nearly twice normal. "Do you mind if I sit down and visit?"

"You're not visiting. You want to take me to the hospital."

"Well, it's true; if someone is sick, sometimes the best place for them is the hospital," I answered, tapping my fingers on the bed stand. "Ruth, can I get you a glass of water? Or make you a cup of tea? Maybe a piece of bread?" I took a closer look at the moldy bread; *maybe that's not such a good idea.*

"No, now go away."

I sat quietly for a moment, unsure how to proceed. "Did you plant the daffodils outside? They're quite beautiful."

Ruth slowly pulled back the sheet and swung a pair of heavy work boots over the side of the bed. She was wearing flannel pajamas with the cartoon image of a skunk adorning the front and back. At a glance, she clearly belonged in the hospital; her eyes were glassy and moist, her color pasty and sallow. She coughed and brought up a rag to her mouth, capturing a large gob of greenish phlegm. Catching her breath, she seemed to relax. "I like daffodils."

"Me too," I replied. "They really brighten up your pathway." I dangled the stethoscope in her direction and asked, "Do you mind? May I take a listen to your lungs?"

In response, she half-turned and I placed the stethoscope against her posterior chest wall. Moist crackles extended from her mid-right lung field up toward the shoulder. The left lung was clear. "It's more than a cold," I said. "You definitely have pneumonia."

"Well, I knew that."

"Well, I'm just saying, I agree with you." I opened my green satchel and fished around for a sterile specimen cup. Perfect, I knew I had one in there somewhere. "Ruth, can you bring up more phlegm and spit it in the cup so that we can identify what kind of bacteria is causing your pneumonia? That way, we can pick the right antibiotic and get you home in just a few days?"

"I need to pee." She lurched to her feet and sat heavily onto a bedside commode at the foot of the bed. I handed her the specimen cup. Almost immediately she coughed and gagged, barely opening the cap in time to spit and wipe her mouth. The effort left her winded. I pressed my case. "Now, I'd like to have officers Mike and John come inside and help you onto a stretcher so that we can get you to town on the fireboat. You'll feel better if we give you some oxygen."

There was another long pause. "Officer John," Ruth finally replied, "he's very nice. He brought my dog Lisa home when she ran away."

For the first time, I was aware that the mop of golden hair curled up beside her pillow was a small dog. I scratched Lisa behind an ear. "John and I can feed Lisa and take her for a walk while you're at the hospital. We'll make sure she's taken good care of." I cracked open the door and waved in the general direction of a flowering forsythia where I knew Mike and Big John were hiding. Meeting them at the door, I explained that, nothing personal, but it might be better if only John came in with the stretcher.

John ducked under the doorway, pulling the stretcher behind. "Hey, it's Lisa!" He reached out a giant, beefy hand and patted the dog lightly on the head. "We'll take good care of her while you're gone."

"You're a tall one, aren't you?" Ruth said.

"Yes, people have noticed that," John answered. "Here, up you go. We're going to take a little ride. You'll be home before you know it." Ruth allowed us to load her onto the stretcher. In a few minutes, she was in the ambulance on low-flow oxygen. I looked at my watch. Change of plans; the ferry left five minutes ago. I'd catch a ride on the fireboat, walk to the car, and with luck make the early afternoon ferry to Chebeague for my afternoon clinic. Fearing the worst (my drawbacks seem to come in twos or threes), I patted my back pocket for my wallet. Empty. Darn. Keys? Good. I have my keys.

Onboard the fireboat, on a blue index billing card, I dutifully wrote down the date, Ruth's full name and diagnosis and tucked it into a compartment to give to Anne the next time I was at the health center. It's concerning how often I forget to bill for house calls. The fireboat transfer went smoothly. As we parted ways on the Portland side, and Ruth transferred from the fireboat to a waiting ambulance, I waved, and she cheerily waved back.

On my way up the coast to catch the Chebeague Island ferry, I picked up Debbie, a part-time nurse from my Portland office. Since I'd cut back to only one clinic day a week on Chebeague, Debbie was the key to a smoother running operation there. She resupplied the clinic, toted out medication samples, confirmed appointments, fit in urgent visits, and importantly, asked patients for their co-pay at the conclusion of a visit.

I liked to chat and could lose track of time during an office visit. Debbie, she was watching the clock. If I was running behind, she might knock on the door and ask to speak to me for a minute. Then she'd run her finger down the schedule and estimate how much time we had for each patient before the late afternoon ferry left for the mainland. "Okay," I'd say, "I need to pick up the pace." That would work for a while until I relapsed back to my old patterns.

Today, lobsterman Ben Shipman came in with his wife, Laurie. His rheumatoid arthritis had continued to improve as I'd titrated his weekly methotrexate up to 25 mg. Last month he'd repainted 200 lobster buoys and changed out the bait bags and lines on 300 traps. I asked him why he was limping, and he rolled up his pants leg. "It's strange, except for this one knee, I'm doing fine. Swelled up like a balloon last week when I came down with a fever and muscle aches."

I arched an eyebrow. Fever and muscle aches don't usually accompany rheumatoid arthritis flareups. Why would his knee be swollen when the rest of his RA was under good control? I had him undress and while examining the knee noticed a red circular rash with central clearing at the base of his neck. "Ticks out yet?" I asked.

"Back yard's full of them. We're constantly doing tick checks on our two boys. They spend more time in the tall grass than they do in bed."

"Well, I need to draw some blood, but I don't think this is an RA flareup. You probably have Lyme arthritis. The rash on the back of your neck fits and the knee is the most common joint to be affected. Can anyone pick up a prescription for you today in town? We'll need to have you on a month of doxycycline." I cracked open the door and asked Debbie to call in the prescription. She opened the shelf where our antibiotic samples were stored and retrieved a sample packet of doxycycline; he can start treatment today. I marveled at her efficiency and made a notation to see Ben next week.

Albion Miller was next. Between the antidepressant medication and the therapeutic light, he'd had the best winter he could recall in ten years. As we talked about titrating the antidepressant down, I noticed an ulcerated lesion the size of a dime on his forearm.

"How long have you had that?" I asked.

"'Bout three months. It keeps healing over and then festering up."

I took out a magnifying glass and looked at it more closely. "I think it's cancerous Albion. It needs to come off. We can get you scheduled for . . . ."

There was a knock on the door. It was Debbie, who'd been listening in. "Your last patient canceled. Even with excising the skin lesion, we should still have time for your house call on the north road and make the ferry."

"Times a wastin'," Albion grinned.

The phone rang. It was officer Mike on Peaks Island. "Hope you don't mind Dr. Radis; Anne gave me your number on Chebeague."

"Mike, that worked out great this morning. Getting Ruth across to Portland was a team effort."

"Well, that's the thing. John and I stayed on Peaks for our shift while you took the fireboat to town. In the ER, I heard they were able to get a chest x-ray that confirmed her pneumonia, and started an IV and ran in a dose of IV antibiotics before the trouble began."

"What kind of trouble?" I asked, as I rose from my stool and stretched the cord out to the empty waiting area.

"Well, Ruth refused to get off the stretcher into a hospital bed."

"Oh, okay. For a moment I thought you were going to tell me she went into respiratory failure or . . . "

"No, but it was a bad scene. Ugly."

"What do you mean?"

"She refused to be admitted. She said it was her right and nobody could make her stay. Now she's home."

"Home?" I slapped my forehead with my palm.

"We're at her cottage. It's a long story, but they finally packed her back in the ambulance, wheeled her back onto the fireboat, and big John and I just dropped her off at her cottage. We have her set up with some oxygen. She's hoping you can stop by tonight on your way home." There was another pause. "She doesn't look good."

Hanging up, I ran my hand through my hair and pulled at one corner of my mustache. *Concentrate.* I gloved up and Debbie handed me a 25-gauge needle filled with lidocaine. After infiltrating the site with the anesthetic, I made an elliptical incision around the skin cancer before undermining the specimen and separated it from the deeper tissues. Then I placed six interrupted sutures of 4-0 Ethilon to close the wound and applied a sterile dressing. With Debbie's help, the procedure took fifteen minutes.

After Albion left, I briefly closed my eyes and reviewed my what-ifs. It might be okay. Maybe Ruth could do better in familiar surroundings at home, with her dog. She'd had a dose of IV antibiotics in the ER. That was good. Perhaps I could convince her to go back on her psychiatric medications. Perhaps. . . my eyes snapped open. What if she took a turn for the worse and still refused to be admitted to the hospital? Worse, what if she died at home? I took a slow, deep breath and exhaled. I'd stop by the cottage on my way home. Opening my pocket calendar, I wrote, *House Call, Ruth.* Then I told myself, *stay sharp; it's going to be a long day.*

13

I n May, I purchased a sixteen-foot C-Dory. Sandi was originally dead set against buying a boat, and that wasn't surprising. Our first boat had sunk several years before on its mooring in a nor'easter, long after most reasonable people had pulled their boats. Okay, all reasonable people. The C-Dory was not quite unsinkable, but it was an upgrade from the center console skiff. For one thing, it had a new engine and a "kicker," a five-horse backup motor. What's more, it had a cuddy cabin to protect me from the wind and a new bilge pump.

Why did Sandi agree to another boat?

Despite cutting back to one day a week on Chebeague, it was clear that my schedule was busier than ever. Hospital admissions were up, and my part-time medical practice in Portland was full tilt. The Peaks clinic was nonstop. Even my weekly Chebeague clinic had picked up. At least three times a week, I was on the 7:15 p.m. ferry or later, and I often arrived home on Peaks Island after the children were in bed.

I didn't know how many times I'd parked the car on the Portland side, raced down Commercial Street for the 5:35 ferry, jacket flapping in the wind, and missed the ferry by less than a minute. I'd fed a lot of quarters into the pay phone outside the Casco Bay Lines terminal, telling Kate and Molly bedtime stories with a heavy dollop of guilt. I was working about seventy hours per week, not counting house calls. Of that seventy hours, I spent more than twelve hours on ferries, driving back and forth to the hospital or to my Portland office.

Of course, I could have stopped admitting patients to the hospital and closed my Portland practice. That would have simplified our life and reduced my hours, but aside from the financial implications, I'd miss the complexity of managing hospitalized patients and the challenge of consulting on outpatients with uncommon disorders. As an internist, I was developing a fascination with rare diseases and how they masquerade as common illnesses. There was an undeniable thrill and satisfaction in making a difficult diagnosis.

Giving up my island practice was equally unpalatable. My National Health Service Corps commitment, which brought me out to the islands in the first place, had been fulfilled, but many of my long-term clinic patients were my friends and neighbors. For the past year and a half, I'd continued my island practice because, well, I enjoyed it. Despite the stress of balancing the Chebeague and Peaks clinics, when the exam door closed and I opened a chart and asked my next patient, "How are you today?" I really wanted to know.

Still, there was an undeniable tension at times between Sandi and me. Our marriage kept on an even keel through the grind of medical school, a year of internship, and three years of my internal medicine residency; but we both thought, naively, that I'd have more control over my hours once I was in private practice. The sessions we'd spent with a marriage counselor a year ago had helped, but my expanding practice had negated the gains we'd made. Sandi had carved out her own quirky niche on Peaks Island in her work as a plumber and had a close circle of friends. She was home to pick up Kate from first grade, and by working part-time, dovetailed Molly's daycare hours with her own. But at times, I knew she felt like a single parent. When I thought about it, and I'll be honest, I wasn't thinking about it nearly enough, I worried that I was following the pattern of my own father's long hours as a chemical engineer and I remembered how little I saw of him during my childhood.

The boat was my commitment to a better work/family balance. I christened her, *SAKAMO*, after SAndi, KAte, and MOlly. Before my first solo voyage to Portland, I jotted a reminder in my pocket planner: *Always wear life preserver. Bring portable marine radio.* Then I turned the key. The engine purred smoothly. Remembering that it was possible for both the main and kicker motor to fail, I opened the pocket planner again: *Buy extra paddle,* and added, *Keep emergency 5-gallon gas onboard.* There. Done. Not quite. *Purchase spare key and hide onboard.*

My friend Obie O'Brien agreed to build me a rowboat I could use to row out to where *SAKAMO* was moored. When it was finished, the simple white dinghy sitting outside his shed was a work of art. Roger, a reclusive neighbor, walked over. As Obie proudly pointed out the features of the dinghy to Roger, from the stainless steel eye-bolt on the bow, to the oak engine mount on the stern, Roger stood silently, wearing a bee veil, his pants held up by a delicate piece of twine. Then Roger said to Obie, "Oarlocks are on backward," and turning to me, he said, "At least it's not a huge, expensive, pointless kind of boat."

SAKAMO did seem to reset our family balance, at least momentarily. On early summer evenings when the bay was flat, the four of us explored nearby islands, pulling the flat-keeled boat up on gravel beaches on an incoming tide. Fort Gorges was an easy trip. So was Ram Island, where hundreds of eiders, herring gulls, and cormorants nested earlier in the summer. We fished for, and sometimes caught, mackerel and sea robin, rock crab and pollock.

On weekends, we walked the Indian trails in the interior of Peaks. The children ran wild along the trail where it followed a shallow, rocky stream, singing and jumping, spooking deer and flushing black ducks and mallards. One night, we hired a babysitter, and Sandi and I rode bicycles around the island and ate ice cream out on the wharf.

A white beluga whale, a rare twelve-foot visitor from Canada, was seen frequently in the bay that summer. The small whale seemed to enjoy associating with people, often swimming alongside sailboats, or poking commercial divers on the shoulder as they collected sea urchins.

A sick leatherback turtle was found in the shallows adjacent to the B&M baked beans plant on the Portland side. Its five-foot prehistoric carapace caught the eye of a passing motorist and turtle specialists drove up from the Boston Aquarium and wrapped the turtle in a moist, protective blanket before driving it to the Boston aquarium for specialized care.

That summer, a public meeting focused on our exploding deer population. Tranquilizing individual animals and transferring them to town was offered as one solution to overpopulation, until another islander reminded the speaker, "You're just spending a lot of money to provide better hunting for mainlanders." In the end, nothing was decided, the same nothing as the past two years.

One Saturday, a squall swept across the bay. At the Trefethen Evergreen Improvement Association, introductory sailboat lessons for eight-twelve-year-olds were in full swing. Before the fleet of single-masted sailboats could make shore, they were tipped over like bowling pins, dumping a dozen children into the water.

A 911 call went out, and the police raced toward Trefethen in their Jeep. Near our house, a boy on a bicycle was pedaling past the Jeep in the opposite direction when a deer ran across the road and collided with the Jeep's windshield. The deer flipped up in the air and knocked the boy off his bike. Big John and his temporary partner, Frank, leaped out of the Jeep to tend to the boy who was remarkably uninjured.

The doe writhed on the pavement, spasmodically trying to stand before collapsing on two fractured legs. Big John said to officer Frank, "It's your turn." That was the first thing I had learned; our police officers are issued revolvers with only one bullet. Big John backed up the crowd and instructed parents to take their children inside. It was time to put the deer out of its misery. Revolver drawn, Frank approached the prostrate, near-death deer and pointed the gun at the its head. Anxiety took hold. He'd never fired his service revolver before. He fired, and missed.

Big John took out his revolver and shot the deer and the two men dragged it to the shoulder. What this meant to the two men's working relationship was anyone's guess. Then they hopped in the Jeep and drove off toward Trefethen. Luckily, by the time they arrived, all of the young sailors had been successfully pulled from the water.

The Jeep accident and the injury to the bicyclist were strong arguments for a controlled hunt on Peaks Island. An emergency meeting was held, but the antihunting faction held firm. Perhaps the argument that might finally swing island sentiment in favor of a hunt was the appearance of Lyme disease on Peaks. The recent Lyme test on Ben Shipman on Chebeague Island came back positive, and that was on an island with a hunting tradition and regular thinning of the herd. Ben was luckier than many Lyme arthritis patients, his knee swelling responded promptly to the course of antibiotics I prescribed. That's not always the case; several of my patients remained unwell six months or more after treatment with mysterious aches and pains, difficulty with concentration, and profound fatigue.

For a month or so, commuting back and forth on *SAKAMO*, I felt more in control of my hours. Then, an unprecedented wave of summer visitors arrived on Peaks, and I extended office hours at the clinic. Admissions at the hospital ticked up. More islanders needed house-calls. I told myself that the increased hours were temporary; that after Labor Day, my hours would track back down, but Sandi was skeptical.

One morning I walked through the door of the Peaks Island Health Center and, in addition to my first two scheduled patients, Sister Mia and Lois Herndon, three new unscheduled patients—including a six-month-old infant awaited me. Anne had explained to them that they had a long wait, but the visitors insisted it was better than taking the ferry to Portland and driving to an urgent care or emergency room.

Sister Mia's visit was a delight. She'd kept to her diet and lost 35 pounds. After a second cortisone shot for her knee last month, she was getting out and walking regularly with the other nuns. I'd been peeling back her diabetic meds to keep up with her improving blood sugars and today, based on a low blood pressure reading, I was stopping one of her three anti-hypertensive medications.

Lois Herndon was not so fortunate. Although I'd tapered her prednisone treatment for giant cell arteritis down to 10 milligrams daily, she had suffered a painful osteoporosis fracture of the lower spine last month while muscling a vacuum cleaner out of the living-room closet. "So much for cleanliness," she said, only half joking. "While you're in town, maybe you can talk with your rheumatology conference friends and schedule a back replacement for me. I feel like a rabbit nibbling on all those pills you're feeding me."

"Lois, I'm reducing the prednisone as quickly as possible. I know you're frustrated, we're both frustrated, but—" Anne knocked on the door and handed me the erythrocyte sedimentation rate (ESR) results. "I have good news for you, the ESR is normal and I want you to reduce the prednisone to 7.5 milligrams daily."

Lois allowed herself a half-smile. "How is my old cat, Isabel?"

I relaxed and leaned back in my seat. "Molly is learning that carrying a cat with its head on her shoulder while the feet drag on the floor makes for a very unhappy cat."

"Did Isabel scratch her?"

"More like a warning scratch; it barely broke the skin." Suddenly, I remembered the waiting room. "I'll see you next month. Please call if the headaches or muscle stiffness recurs on the lower dose prednisone. Once I can safely reduce the prednisone to 5 milligrams daily, you should start losing some of that excess weight and feel more like your old self."

Lois leaned on her cane as she struggled to her feet. She caught a glimpse of herself in the mirror and gasped, "My god, I look hideous. I'm a blimp."

While Lois arranged for a follow-up visit and I scribbled a note in her chart, Johnny Dinsmore limped through the front door. He caught a glimpse of me and pointed to his foot. I thought, *Gout management is straightforward. Why in the world am I seeing this foot every month?* Johnny settled into a chair, took off his shoe, and propped his foot up on the magazine table.

Ruth, my schizophrenic patient who survived her pneumonia at home, followed Johnny in. She plopped down in the one remaining seat and though it was 80 degrees out, wiggled out of the first of three sweaters she wore beneath a tattered parka. Then she pointed to Johnny and his swollen foot and stage whispered, "I know what you have. It's the gout, and I know what to do. You should eat black cherries, a lot of them." Satisfied, she hummed a hymn that was in tune, even if oddly out of place.

"How many cherries?" Johnny asked. Evidently, he was considering her advice. After all, he'd seen me for the gout and here he was with another attack.

"Six cherries when you first feel the burn, and so forth and so on . . ." She waved her hand dismissively.

The summer visitors' illnesses were straightforward. Both the mother and six-month old tested positive for strep throats. A young diabetic presented with a draining ulcer on her forearm. I took a deep culture of the drainage and wrote her family doctor's name and address on the lab slip so she would get a copy. The woman was leaving for Indiana in the morning and I prescribed a broad-spectrum antibiotic to get her started.

Anne roomed Johnny next, and I anticipated his black cherry question by bringing up the topic myself. "Another gout attack?" I shook my head sadly at the massively swollen great toe. "You are, of course, taking the allopurinol daily?"

"Well . . . there may be times . . . "

"And the colchicine? You take it as soon as you feel an attack coming on?"

"Colchicine? You mean to say I'm supposed to . . . "

"That's unusual," I said, cutting him short and shaking my head quizzically. "You're taking both the allopurinol and colchicine as prescribed and still having attacks. Your gout needs a boost. Here's what I suggest: Purchase a pill box and place one allopurinol inside for each day of the week. On the outside of the box with a magic marker write, *If gout attack, take 6 black cherries and 1 colchicine. Repeat in 1 hour.* Black cherries, they're your ace in the hole."

Johnny nodded his head approvingly. "That's the ticket! I think we're onto something now!"

"Now, of course, you need to stay on track with the allopurinol and remember the colchicine," I continued. "The cherries may be all that's lacking. Now, how about a shot for that toe?"

Following the shot, Johnny exchanged a knowing glance with Ruth as he limped by to make a follow-up appointment at the front desk. Anne handed me Ruth's half-empty vial of Thorazine while I scribbled a note on Johnny at my desk. I emptied out the vial and slowly counted out the remaining pills before subtracting the total from the date of her last prescription. Perfect. She's taking the medication every day. As I chatted with her, she seemed perfectly appropriate. I asked if she was hearing any voices, and she answered coyly, "I hear your voice."

"I recently passed along the remedy of black cherries you recommended. Do you approve?" I asked.

"Yes . . . Yes, we certainly do." Ruth smiled broadly, clearly pleased with herself.

Hmmm, I thought, the two of us might not be alone. While a higher dose of Thorazine might extinguish the background voices, it could also trigger over-sedation or occasionally a more serious side-effect called Tardive dyskinesia accompanied by random movements of the tongue and large muscle groups. After Ruth left, I opened my pocket calendar and wrote: *Call psychiatry re Ruth. Leave well enough alone?*

There was a commotion in the waiting room. A close friend, Kay Taylor, huddled inside the doorway with her dog, Moxie. The dog was drooling; a large soup bone was wrapped around her lower jaw, and Kay was in tears. As I watched from my desk, Moxie whimpered and clawed at the bone and turned herself around in tight circles. It was a pitiful sight.

The waiting room was temporarily empty, and before Kay could ask, I offered, "Quickly, come in. I'll take a look at Moxie." Kay and Anne led the miserable animal into the back room.

I donned a pair of sterile gloves and bent down to examine the soup bone as Kay straddled Moxie and grasped her collar. *This shouldn't be too difficult.* Moxie was a medium-sized older dog, with gray flecks on her muzzle and short brown hair. I looked into Moxie's eyes; nothing malevolent there. The bone seemed to be lodged behind the lower canines. I lightly jiggled the bone and Moxie yelped and snapped at my hand, narrowly missing my index finger.

"That was close," I exhaled, now even more determined to remove the soup bone.

"I'm sorry, Chuck," Kay said. "Moxie is usually a gentle, even-tempered dog; we'll take the ferry to town. She was rooting around in the garbage bin and the next thing we knew the soup bone was wrapped around her lower jaw. Our vet says he handles these kinds of problems all the time."

"Did he say what he gives to calm the dog down?" I asked, unwilling to admit defeat.

"Demerol. He gives them a 35-milligram shot of Demerol." Kay handed me the telephone message from the vet. "Why?"

"I have Demerol in the office. Let's give Moxie a shot. I'll see another patient or two and over lunch, then we'll give it another go."

Kay's eyes brightened, "Oh, you're a life saver. Our vet's office is an hour's drive north of Portland, and it would mean so much."

After the injection into her hind leg, Moxie curled up on the floor by my desk and promptly fell asleep. I checked on her between patients and lightly pulled open an eyelid which promptly drooped shut. After lunch, Kay gently helped her drowsy pet to a standing position while I re-gloved and grabbed a pair of wire cutters from the basement. Then

Kay straddled Moxie and pulled the leash tight and whispered, "Ready." As I reached out and touched the soup-bone, Moxie's eyes flashed open like fire hydrants, and she jerked her head to the side and somehow bit Kay's hand. I jumped back, landing on my rear, and dropped the wire-cutters, barely eluding Moxie's gnashing teeth. Kay's jeans were torn and blood dripped onto the carpet.

Then, Moxie promptly laid down and fell asleep.

Later, the next day, I took it as a point of pride when I learned that Kay's vet had to resort to general anesthesia and a hack saw to remove the soup bone from Moxie's lower jaw. Even so, before bed, I took out my pocket calendar and wrote: *No more Dr. Doolittle!*

A dense, raw fog hung over the bay. I slid my dingy down the beach and pushed off toward *SAKAMO*, a hundred yards offshore. Halfway to the mooring, our cottage disappeared in the mist. Herring gulls squawked and wheeled overhead as I rowed by a group of dusky brown female eiders cooing to a raft of bobbing chicks.

As I approached my boat, a common tern hovered over the water before dropping like a stone and emerging a moment later, its beak dripping with fish. A juvenile osprey banked toward the eiders, but the odds of a meal were apparently low because the bird pulled up and disappeared into the mist. Reaching *SAKAMO*, I tied-up the dinghy and clambered aboard, started the engine, and released the mooring line.

I motored toward the ferry landing. Forgetting about the stress of navigating a small boat in pea-soup fog, I'd simply follow the Machigonne's wake to Portland. Hugging the shoreline, intent on staying out of the busy main channel, I spotted a deer in the water. Only the past week, as I worked in the yard, a 6-point buck had raced by me and plunged into the ocean. Curious, I jumped into my rowboat and followed the animal as it made a beeline for Little Diamond Island. The buck swam effortlessly, its antlered head like a figurehead on the prow of a ship, until it reached the far shore, shook itself off, and disappeared into the woods.

Not all deer have a plan. *The Portland Press Herald* had recently reported a fishing boat coming across a deer swimming five miles off the coast in the general direction of Great Britain. The crew lassoed the exhausted deer and brought it on board. Where they released it is anyone's guess. I hope it wasn't on Peaks Island; we have enough deer, thank you.

I turned my attention back to the water and cringed as *SAKAMO* glided over an abandoned sewer outfall pipe a few feet beneath the surface. Instinctively, I pulled back on the throttle and adjusted the tilt controls on the engine, raising the prop away from the obstruction. I'd forgotten how shallow the water was this close to shore, and my carelessness almost resulted in a mangled prop. Opening my chart, I marked the area with a red magic marker, and double checked my course to the ferry landing, about a half-mile away.

The sight of the outfall pipe was a reminder that the bay was far less polluted than when we'd moved to Peaks four years before. At the time, it wasn't unusual to see floating feces and toilet paper drifting on the water from dozens of illegal discharge pipes. Only a handful of clam flats on the upper reaches of Casco Bay were open to clamming. Since a water treatment plant had been constructed on Peaks and city officials clamped down on illegal discharge, the quality of water in the bay had improved dramatically. This summer, we'd received welcome news; the bacterial count in the water in front of our house was nearly zero and we could safely eat the clams we dug.

A few minutes later, the outlines of the *Machigonne* emerged from the fog. I idled off to one side as the deckhands slid the gangplank onboard and the ferry backed away from the wharf. Then I tucked in behind, and opened my thermos of coffee, enjoying the solitude. Off Fort Gorges, the *Machigonne* slowed and emitted a series of long blasts and I pulled back on the throttle. Off to port, a young woman in a kayak waved to the captain aboard the *Machigonne*, unmindful that even on radar she was nearly invisible on the water. I realized that if I was motoring by myself in the dense fog, her low silhouette would have been impossible to see until the last moment. Bobby Emerson, my island connection to the lobster industry, had complained to me recently: "If I hit one of those kayaks in the fog, it would feel like a little tap on the bow, a speed bump."

Arriving in town, I docked and walked down Commercial Street to my car. The fog was breaking up by the time I exited the parking lot. I checked my watch; two hours, more than enough time to round on my four patients at the hospital before heading to Chebeague Island. Heading upstairs after dropping off the health center specimens at the lab, I reviewed the chart of an admission I'd picked up through the emergency room the previous night, while the third-year family practice resident presented the case.

"Let me say this," the resident looked up from his notes. "I have no idea what's wrong with this lady," which was both refreshing and a little disturbing. To be honest, after hearing the thumbnail presentation from the ER attending last night and agreeing to accept the admission, I had no idea what was wrong either. "So, she owns an organic farm with her husband," the resident began, "and she's been unwell for the better part of three months. The fevers came first, usually in the evening. She took her temperature a few times, and it scared her, so she stopped. In the ER last night," the resident checked her notes, "she was 103.2."

"Do they own cattle or pigs?" I asked, aware that farmers are susceptible to zoonotic infections such as salmonella and campylobacter.

"No, I asked her about that. They grow mostly vegetables. They have contracts with a number of the local restaurants; it's a farm-to-table deal. Anyway, when the fevers settled in, she developed a sore throat and intermittent aching in her wrists. After a few weeks, she saw her family doctor and he ran some tests. I have copies here. Strep culture negative, mono-spot, urine culture all negative, chest x-ray normal. The only thing out of line was a CBC with a white count of 17,500 and a borderline anemia, so he prescribed a course of antibiotics, thinking this was a bacterial infection. "Nothing changed."

"Travel?" I was writing down a differential diagnosis.

"No, they're homebodies. She saw her family doctor again, and because of the fevers and wrist pain, he picked up blood cultures, a rheumatoid factor, an ANA, and a sedimentation rate to assess for inflammation. The rheumatoid factor and ANA were negative, but the sedimentation rate was 106." The resident paused and admitted, "That's the highest sed rate I've ever seen."

"The sedimentation rate of a patient of mine last year was 116," I said, thinking back to Lois Herndon and her diagnosis of giant cell arteritis. "Headaches? Jaw pain? Visual changes?"

"No, none of that; I did wonder about giant cell arteritis," the resident added. "Do you think that's worth checking on?"

"Wrong age. She's in her late thirties. People under the age of 60 don't develop giant cell arteritis. Anything else?"

"No, except maybe her wrists are a little swollen," the resident added.

I stepped into the room and extended a hand. Nora Crothers was a strikingly robust appearing woman with calloused hands and a streak of premature gray in her hazel hair where it was pulled back in a ponytail. "Good morning, Mrs. Crothers."

"Nora is fine. You just missed my husband. You're seeing me at my best. Right now, I could jump up and pick a row of greens, but wait till this afternoon and I'll be a mess."

"That's what I understand." I sat down on the edge of the bed and examined her fingernails for splinter hemorrhages, a sign of possible endocarditis—a heart valve infection, and a cause of unexplained fevers. The nails appeared normal. Nora grimaced as I flexed and extended the wrists.

"It doesn't make sense. My husband has taken on the harvesting while I'm getting over . . . whatever this is, and I'm like a lady of leisure. I can't believe I'm here in the hospital." I quietly auscultated her heart and lungs, and methodically examined her eyes, mouth, lymph nodes, abdomen, skin, and joints. Except for slightly reddened tonsils, and equivocal swelling in the wrists, her exam was normal.

"Mrs. Crothers, when a fever lasts this long and there's no clear explanation after routine testing, we call it an FUO, a fever of unknown origin. Viral infections can trigger fevers, but they usually resolve over weeks, not months. I'm going to ask one of the infectious disease specialists to stop by and see you, repeat your blood cultures when you spike a fever, and later this morning you'll be going down to radiology for a CT scan of your abdomen and pelvis."

"Do you think it could be cancer?" her eyes sharpened. "My mother had lymphoma."

I chose my words carefully. "People with fever associated with cancer often lose weight, and your weight has been stable. Your exam doesn't suggest cancer, but yes, we have to keep that possibility in mind, that's part of the reason I'm ordering the CT scan of your abdomen and pelvis. We'll get to the bottom of this." I closed her chart and stood to go. On her bed stand was a vase filled with fresh-cut summer flowers: daylilies, Queen Anne's lace, yarrow, and chicory. I brushed my hand against the display and identified a sprig of orange-flowered hawkweed hidden from view. "From your farm?" I asked.

"My husband picked them from the edge of the field early this morning. He says we can deal with anything once we have a diagnosis. I believe that."

By the time I arrived back at the Portland waterfront, the fog had lifted and a dozen sailboats skimmed across the inner bay. I pointed *SAKAMO* toward Chebeague Island, six miles to the northeast, taking care to stay well to the west of an unmarked ledge extending off the shore of Great Diamond Island. The afternoon flew by, with asthma and emphysema patients and blood pressure checks and sore throats at the Chebeague clinic. I congratulated a type II diabetic for eliminating soda in her diet and switching to diabetic candy. She'd lost six pounds, and the simple changes, combined with walking to the post office each day, significantly improved her blood sugars. The next patient, A 68-year-old woman, was concerned about light-headedness when she went for her daily walk. I auscultated a worrisome heart murmur consistent with aortic stenosis. After the next patient cancelled, I talked over my findings with Charlie Hoag in cardiology, who agreed the findings were worrisome. He'd see her as soon as an echocardiogram of the heart could be scheduled.

By 3:45 there was no one left in the waiting area. A few minutes later I was back aboard *SAKAMO*. A bank of leaden clouds gathered to the west as I raced for home against a line of whitecaps. A flock of Wilson's storm-petrels fluttered into the wave troughs, their feet skimming the water as if they were tap dancing. Oblivious to *SAKAMO*, the swallow-sized birds darted to the left and right of the bow. I slowed to headway speed. In another moment, like fallen leaves, they scattered with the wind as suddenly as they'd appeared.

When the storm hit, I was less than a mile from home. As I approached my mooring in the driving rain, I cut the engine and tried to pick up my mooring pennant with a boat hook. On the third pass, now thoroughly soaked, I caught the pennant and attached the line to the bow cleat. Then, instead of climbing into the rowboat, I waited out the storm in the cuddy cabin. Most thunderstorms, even large ones, dissipate as they cross over the cool waters of the bay, and this storm was no exception. In another fifteen minutes, the torrential rain was replaced by a faint drizzle before the skies cleared to the west and a brilliant double rainbow appeared over the island.

I waved my arms from the boat hoping that Sandi might see me from the kitchen table, and I was in luck. She came down to the beach with Molly and Kate. The sun peeked below the receding storm clouds. As I rowed to shore, I shouted, "Look behind you!" and the three of them turned to see the rainbow above the hillside.

I pulled the rowboat up above the high tide beach grass and flipped it over. By then, the rainbow was fading, the sharp bright colors dissipating into muted pastels. Aa few minutes later, Molly asked, "Who took the rainbow?"

Dinner was barely underway when there was a knock on the door. Behind the screen door was a gaunt, tall man I'd never seen before. My hair was still damp from a hot shower and I wore a faded T-shirt. Still chewing on a slice of pizza, I asked, "What can I do for you?"

"Well," the man ran his hand through a mop of red hair, "That's the thing, I'm not altogether sure. You see, my wife thought I should come and see you. I have some abdominal pain, well it's not actually pain, more a discomfort, and instead of ignoring it, she suggested I make sure I'm okay, check it out. We're renting the blue cottage up by the tennis courts. By the way, thank you for seeing me. Roger. Roger Wilson."

"I see," I said, shaking his hand tentatively, my suspicion growing that there was a point of contention between him and his wife, and I was going to somehow pay for their disagreement. "So, what is it exactly that she feels can't wait until the clinic opens tomorrow morning?"

"It's my abdomen, but right now I'm feeling a bit better. It's not like I've never had pain before. When I get back to the house we're renting, I'll tell her that you've told me it can wait till tomorrow."

"Let's be clear here; I haven't said any such thing," I replied sharply. There was something both ingratiating and disagreeable about the man. From time to time, island neighbors knock on our door for after-hour assistance, and that's perfectly reasonable. Some illnesses or injuries are not quite emergencies but shouldn't wait until the next day to evaluate. But this was something else, a visitor wanting me to reassure him that nothing was seriously wrong, impinging on precious family time. On the other hand, now that he was at our door, I couldn't simply send him away. I asked, "What exactly is going on with your abdomen?"

"I have Crohn's disease, had maybe a half-dozen surgeries, and early this afternoon I began to bloat up. Vomited, maybe once, maybe two or three times. My wife said, 'Let's catch the ferry to town and you can get checked out in the emergency room.' I said, 'No, the last thing I want to do is go to the emergency room.'"

The man looked unwell. Now that I was giving him my full attention, I noticed that his breath had the fetid smell of small bowel bile. A small bowel obstruction can do that. I glanced back into the kitchen. Sandi and Kate and Molly were at the table spooning out a carton of ice cream into their bowls. I could almost taste my desert. Sandi shot me a glance: *How long? A minute? An hour?*

Mr. Wilson seemed to suppress a gag and burped. There it was again, an altogether unpleasant, bilious odor. Sandi vacated the kitchen with the children as I led Mr. Wilson inside. He grimaced as he settled onto the bench, the same bench and table Sandi's family sat around for dinner on the dairy farm she grew up on. "So, tell me about your Crohn's disease, oh, and while you're at it, here's a pen. I'd appreciate it if you would write down your name, birthdate, and home address. I'll have my office assistant call you tomorrow for your health insurance information."

"Well, there's really not much to say. When my Crohn's flares, I take some kind of medication, which sometimes works, but other times I end up in the hospital with a surgery. They've been trying to get me to take a daily bunch of pills, but, well, I ran out of them a few weeks ago." He stopped, as if this was all I needed to know. Perhaps it was all he knew.

". . . and you've required several surgeries? Bowel obstructions?"

"Yes, four." As yet, he had not even written his name down.

I held off on getting a full history. I realized that my job was *not* to make a definitive diagnosis; to do so would require laboratory and radiographic testing and the skills of an experienced surgeon. My job was to either reassure Mr. Wilson and his wife that his abdominal pain could wait till morning, or insist that he go to town tonight. So far, I was leaning heavily toward the latter. I looked at the wooden bench at the kitchen table and said, "Let's have you lie you down on the couch and I'll take a look."

Inside the living room, Sandi and the children were watching a Disney movie. As I entered with Mr. Wilson, she shot me a sharp glance, turned the TV off, and marched Kate and Molly upstairs for a bath.

With some difficulty, Mr. Wilson lay down on the couch and lifted up his T-shirt. His abdomen was a distended roadmap of surgical scars: an oblique incision ran along the right lower ribs consistent with a gall bladder surgery; a 2-inch incision in the lower right quadrant—probably from an appendectomy; a long mid-line incision, probably an exploratory surgery for an obstructed bowel. I pressed my stethoscope against the abdominal wall and although bowel sounds were present, they were clearly diminished. Palpating his abdomen, his pain seemed to localize to the left lower quadrant.

Helping him up, I was brief and concise: "You need to go to the emergency room. You need blood work and an ultrasound of the abdomen at a minimum; probably a CT scan as well. You may have an early obstruction or a case of diverticulitis, or perhaps your Crohn's needs urgent treatment, but I don't think it's something you can ride out at your cottage on the island tonight. Bowels can perforate and that's extremely serious. If you get your things together quickly, you won't need to take the emergency fireboat; you can make the evening ferry to Portland tonight."

Mr. Wilson pulled down his T-shirt and buckled up his pants. "I was afraid you'd say that. I sure would like to wait and be seen at my hometown hospital. They know me there." At the screen door, he asked one last time, "You don't think I can wait until morning?"

I shook my head. "No."

"Well, we'll see how it goes. I do appreciate it. Thank you."

In another moment, he was out the door. The information I asked him to fill out was blank. All I remembered was that his name was Bob. Even so, I took out a scrap paper and wrote down my physical findings and recommendations, dated it, and filed it away in my desk. The specter of a malpractice suit hovered on the edge of my mind.

The children crept back downstairs and Sandi turned on the TV. Sandi sat on the far edge of the couch, Molly on her lap, and Kate wiggled in between us. The phone rang—we're in the Island Phone Directory—and I stepped back into the kitchen. It was Mrs. Wilson wanting to know what I thought; her husband refused to go to town. I could feel a burst of anger welling up before realizing the poor woman lived with his denial every day. I softened my voice and repeated my advice that the two of them take the ferry to Portland and go to the nearest emergency room. "If he refuses to go to Portland and decompensates during the night, if you call 911, the police will come to the house and arrange for a transfer on the fireboat."

Hanging up, I joined Sandi upstairs and helped put the girls to bed. Afterward, we lay in bed, each of us alone in our thoughts. Sandi lay on her side, facing away from me. I reached out a hand and rested it on her hip and wondered where to start. "Chuck," Sandi turned back to me, "I think we need to go to counseling again. What we're doing now isn't working. I know you're trying, but now we can't even have an undisturbed dinner with you. There was a short silence before she said, "I think we should both go."

"I'll go. I'll definitely go," I said immediately.

"That's good. Most husbands wouldn't. I'll call the counselor tomorrow," she answered. Then she curled toward me and lay her head against my shoulder. A few minutes later, a soft, gentle hum told me she was asleep.

14

After nearly a week in the hospital, the cause of Nora Crothers' fever remained elusive. Her drenching sweats and fever of unknown origin (FUO) spiked each evening and returned to normal each morning. There'd been no growth on cultures of her blood, urine, or cervix. Her chest x-ray and CT scans of the abdomen and pelvis were normal. So was a bone-marrow evaluation. Cancer seemed unlikely. At her last blood draw, her repeat ESR rose to 122, breaking Lois Herndon's previous record of 116 at the onset of her giant cell arteritis. I made a mental note to tell Lois she was no longer the record holder. She'd appreciate the gallows humor, particularly since she was finally shedding some of her prednisone side-effects.

A few minutes before my arrival that morning, Ms. Crothers developed an aching sensation in her chest. The resident ordered an EKG, and I reviewed the tracing on my way into the room. The EKG was clearly abnormal, but not suggestive of a myocardial infarction. I placed my stethoscope on her chest and listened. A patient in the adjacent bed had the TV on. A nurse was speaking to another nurse while she adjusted an IV rate. The phone rang.

"Shut the TV off. Can everyone be quiet for a moment?" I said over the din.

"What's wrong with Dr. Radis? He doesn't have to yell," the taller nurse whispered as she turned the TV off and left the room.

I closed my eyes and tried to clear my mind. Yell? Did I just yell? I don't usually yell. I was frustrated that my patient didn't have a diagnosis. I was concerned that Sandi was upset with me. I wished there were more hours in the day to play with Kate and Molly. A blanket of silence settled over the room. I placed my stethoscope on Nora Crothers' chest. The heart sounds were regular. There was no murmur. But there, between the beats, was a faint sound like two pieces of leather rubbing together. Pericarditis. An ultrasound should confirm that there was fluid in the sac around the heart. Okay, at least I had a partial explanation for the fevers.

I still was unable to put the pieces together: the high white blood count and sedimentation rate, the painful wrists, the friction rub of pericarditis. Silently, I reviewed my working differential diagnosis; nothing seemed to explain the diverse features of Nora Crothers' illness. I needed more help.

That's when I realized, if I hurried, I could make the weekly rheumatology conference across town at Maine Medical Center. Fifteen minutes later, I quietly entered the conference room and sat at a rear table as a case of lupus was discussed. Senior attending rheumatologist Paulding Phelps asked, "Any more cases?" Then he noted my presence at the back, "Dr. Radis, do you have something interesting for us?"

After presenting my case, several ideas emerged from the group. The first was that I was in the right room, my patient's illness almost certainly represented a rheumatologic illness. One rheumatologist suspected my patient's illness could represent an immune reaction to a chronic hepatitis B or C infection. Another suggested I order a CT angiogram of the abdomen to evaluate for occult vasculitis. "Rheumatoid arthritis? If you haven't seen rheumatoid arthritis trigger pericarditis and fevers and localized joint inflammation," one rheumatologist suggested, "you haven't seen enough rheumatoid arthritis." In shorthand, I entered the ideas in my pocket calendar: *Call resident: hep B/C serology, order angio, CCP antibodies.*

Paulding Phelps hung back until the others were finished. "Those are all good suggestions. One thing more, Dr. Radis, have you rounded on the patient in the evening when she has her fever?"

I admitted, I hadn't.

"Well, it may be prudent to do so. A patient with this kind of history may have an evanescent rash with the high fever. That would be pathognomonic of—"

"Adult onset Still's disease," another rheumatologist listening in nodded. "That would make sense."

"There's no test that confirms the disease, but if the characteristic rash is present with the fever, that would clinch the diagnosis," Dr.

Phelps continued. "Anyway, that's where my vote goes. Good luck. Tough case."

I thanked the group. Perfect. Before closing the pocket planner, I glanced at my messages from the previous day. All of them were checked off. All of them but one: *Marriage counseling tomorrow 11.*

Shoot. I flew out the conference room and ran to the car. The office of the marriage counselor was located on Forest Avenue. It wasn't far, but I was already late. In front of a CVS pharmacy, I parked and jumped out of the car and was halfway to the counselor's office building when something clicked in my subconscious: The car was running. Fortunately, when I retraced my steps, the car was also unlocked. Taking the steps two at a time, I burst into the waiting room. It was empty. The receptionist was on the phone but lifted up her finger for me to wait. In a few minutes she opened up the glass slider and asked, "Dr. Radis?"

"Yes."

"Your wife is in with the counselor. She said you're welcome to join them." The receptionist buzzed me in and pointed to the second door on the left. I knocked on the door and ran a hand through my hair. Okay, maybe it's better this way; I don't have time to think.

The counselor, a willowy, gray-haired woman with the settled presence of a yoga instructor opened the door. "We're so glad you could make it . . ."

"Sorry I'm late." I peered past her and there was Sandi on the couch. She was in tears. I sheepishly sat down, trying to gauge how close was okay. In response, she reached out and took my hand. I took a slow, deep breath and exhaled.

"Chuck, we were just talking about how difficult, I might say frenetic, your schedule is, and looking at ways both of you can accommodate those hours or work to improve them. I remember when we met last year that Sandi agreed to let go of her expectation you'd be home regularly for dinner. That was difficult; dinner was the one time everyone in her family came together on the dairy farm. There was a lot of laughter. It's one of her happier memories. You promised to be more aware of choices you were making. Do you remember that?"

"I do. I was on several hospital committees. I dropped off those committees."

"But every time you make a change, something else takes its place," Sandi said as she dropped my hand and fidgeted with the barrette in her hair. "And you conveniently forget how often you come home at eight or nine at night. How many times, in the past two weeks, have you caught the 5:35 ferry home?"

"I'm taking my boat lately."

"Fine. How many times have you walked in the door before seven in the past two weeks?"

I didn't answer right off and drummed a finger on the magazine table. "I don't know. I would guess, five, maybe six."

Sandi took out a yellow sheet of paper. "What would you say if I told you that I've written down the times you arrive home by seven, and it's twice. Twice, in the past two weeks, not five times. Most of the time, it's later, much later. Kate and Molly are in bed. They won't go to sleep until you come home. They watch for you coming down the walkway. And yes, you are very good about going upstairs and telling them stories, but by then they're exhausted. They need their sleep."

"I know you're right," I answered. "But getting the boat has helped. Think about the ferries I used to miss. This summer has been crazy, but in a few weeks, we should see a real difference. The Peaks clinic should slow down; right now, nearly half of the patients I see are summer visitors. It should get better."

"And what about next summer?" Sandi asked. "And the summer after that? After the first three years it was going to be better when you stopped going to Long Island and Cliff Island for house calls. This spring it was going to be better when you bought SAKAMO. People like you. They want you to be their doctor. Every time you say 'yes' again to your patients, you're saying 'no' to your family."

Afterwards, we went out for lunch and tried to continue the conversation. Our conversation was forced; we missed the mediation of the counselor. She reframed our questions and followed up on our replies. And she was fair. I didn't feel she was on Sandi's side or my side; she was trying to help us see a way forward. I looked at my watch, it was time for Sandi to take the 12:45 ferry back to Peaks to pick up Molly at the babysitters.

Driving toward the waterfront, a heavy, impenetrable fogbank closed in. I dropped Sandi off at the dock. Sandi checked her purse for a ticket and leaned into my window and gave me a kiss goodbye. Before she disappeared inside the *Machigonne*, she turned and smiled. I realized, then, that I needed to do more; if I wanted our marriage to succeed, I needed to fight for it. It was my turn to cry.

I realized it wasn't safe to take *SAKAMO* up the coast. Between the fog, my absent mindedness, and our therapy, I'd be lucky to get out of Portland harbor before I hit a ledge. I'd have to drive up the coast, catch the ferry to Chebeague Island for my afternoon clinic, and stop off at the hospital to see Nora Crothers on my way home.

No clinic day is routine, but today, there were no surprises, and aware that I was still upset, I focused even more than usual on each patient visit and carefully dictated my findings and recommendations. On my way back to the hospital, the counseling session weighed on me. Was it true that by saying "yes" to my patients, I was saying "no" to my family? The criticism seemed an oversimplification of my work and my relationship to Sandi and the children. Medicine is not a nine-to-five avocation. Out of balance? I parked the truck in the hospital lot and sat for a moment. Yes. Absolutely. My work/family balance was tilted toward work, lots of it, more than I could (or should) sustain indefinitely.

Entering through the emergency room entrance, I stopped at the doctor's dining room and sat for a moment, sipping on my fourth cup of coffee of the day, a wave of fatigue washing over me. An oncologist grabbed a bag of chips, shouted hello, and was out the door. Divorced. A pulmonary specialist entered and sat nursing a can of Coca Cola. Pending divorce. A half-dozen family practice physicians came in from the cafeteria and set down their trays. One, I knew was divorced, another was in a second marriage. Of the other four, one was single, and three, from what little I'd heard, seemed to have solid marriages. The operative word was "seemed." Who really knows what goes on in a marriage?

I'd never considered that divorce might be in Sandi's and my future. But I would guess neither had my physician peers. The Chinese proverb I applied to my mental health patients now spoke clearly to me: *If we don't change the direction we're headed, we'll end up where we are going.*

Upstairs, I reviewed the chart of Nora Crothers. Her nurse flagged me down. "Your patient's fever just spiked to 104 degrees. Do you want blood cultures drawn?

"Yes. I'll enter an order. Can you call lab, and have them come up and draw two sets of blood cultures, twenty minutes apart?"

"Done. Restart antibiotics?"

"No," I said, "Not yet." I was tempted to start prednisone. Prednisone is a perfectly reasonable treatment for pericarditis. The likelihood that her fevers were driven by an occult infection was nearly zero. I was aware of a tongue-in-cheek definition of a rheumatologist circulating in my own doctor's dining room: *A clinician who comes to the bedside, orders a lot of tests that come back inconclusive and treats the patient with steroids.*

I closed the chart and paused at the open door of Nora Crothers' room. Her cheeks were flushed and her hair stringy and soaked in sweat. She leaned forward, groaning, and clenched a fist against her chest. She noticed me lingering by the door. "Dr. Radis, how are you today?" She was the sickest patient I'd managed in months and she was asking *me* how I was doing? Some people are just born nice.

I retrieved my stethoscope from my green satchel and pressed it lightly against her chest. The heart was racing at more than a hundred beats per minute, and the leathery friction rub sounded like sandpaper. As I opened the back of her hospital gown to listen to the lungs, I silently thanked Paulding Phelps. There it was, in all its textbook glory: the rash of Still's disease. The salmon-colored, irregular, blotchy rash stretched across the upper back, into both upper arms, and over the upper abdomen. When I pointed out the rash on her upper arms, Nora said, "Rash? I haven't noticed any rash. I'm not allergic to the bed sheets, am I?"

"No, it's the missing piece of the puzzle. The appearance of the rash with the daily fever, along with the joint pain, and the pericarditis, fits with a disorder called adult onset Still's disease. As yet, the trigger remains a mystery. I want to begin an infusion of Solumedrol tonight. It's a relative of prednisone and the primary treatment for your disease. I think you'll feel better soon."

I toned down any sense of enthusiasm I had over making the diagnosis. Whether Still's disease afflicted young children, where it was most common, or adults, the textbooks described patients who required high-dose prednisone treatment indefinitely. A small percentage of patients died from complications of the disease. I decided that this was one case where I'd initiate treatment, but then refer her to Dr. Phelps in rheumatology.

I wrote the orders for Solumedrol, dropped off the Chebeague Island patient laboratory specimens, and a few minutes later was on my way to the waterfront. Now that I was finished with rounds, the day came racing back: the Chebeague clinic, the counseling session, Sandi waving goodbye, the rash of Still's disease, the realization that I needed to make real change in my practice. I pulled over at a convenience store parking lot and shut off the car. Then I spied a pay phone booth and called one of my physician friends.

I told him that I was okay, well not really okay, but hoped he could cover for me tonight. I bit the inside of my lip, hoping he wouldn't ask too many questions. When he said, "yes," I signed out my hospital patients. Then he laughed and said, "Phone coverage for the islands too? I get some impossible phone calls from your patients. I mean what am I going to do?"

"Yes, the islands, too. Thank you so much," I said and hung up the phone.

There was one last hurdle to overcome. I was in no condition to take *SAKAMO* home in the fog. As I walked down the wharf to the Casco Bay Lines, I picked up a newspaper off a bench and decided that if a book wasn't enough to discourage medical questions, perhaps a newspaper held up to my nose might do the trick. I boarded the ferry, took the first seat on the inside bench, and opened the newspaper to the sports section. The ferry pulled away into the fog. I glanced out the window; a solitary heron kept pace with the boat, its wings dappling the quiet surface of the water, and I felt myself relax.

Thirty minutes later, the diesel engines throttled down and two crewmen slid open the lower doors and prepped the gangplank for off-loading. Head down, I gathered my backpack and green satchel and wearily joined the other passengers waiting to disembark, staring straight ahead as the line moved slowly forward. Passengers drifted off the wharf on bicycles or trudged up a dirt road toward a house I didn't recognize. In another moment, I was alone.

Then it hit me. Through a gap in the fog, Peaks Island was clearly visible across the channel. I was on Little Diamond Island. Somehow, in my stupor, I'd boarded the wrong ferry, the down-the-bay ferry. This was not my island. I was too numb to yell or stamp my feet or throw my backpack on the ground. I stood dumbly on the wharf. Then, from up the channel, I could see the faint outlines of a substantial boat. It was Dave Quinby's work boat, and I flapped my arms like a giant pigeon, hoping he'd look my way. No reaction. I cupped my hands and yelled and whistled. Dave peered over the wheel inside the pilot house, focused over the bow, intent on safely navigating the fog toward his mooring off the western shore of Peaks. The Quinby boat slipped by, the roar of the diesels drowning out my hopes for a quick ride home.

Behind the pilot house, on a fish crate, sat Kip, age five, nearly asleep. She drowsily looked up toward the wharf and, recognizing me, smiled and waved. I pantomimed a knock on the pilot door and pointed to the Little Diamond wharf and then to her dad. She cocked her head and looked at me curiously. Why was Kate's dad doing a crazy dance?

Then she ever so slowly pushed herself off the crate and brushed off her pants and picked up her rag doll and opened the pilot door and disappeared inside. I held my breath. The metal work boat made a slow, lazy turn to port and glided back to the Little Diamond wharf.

16

F all. On a moonless, starlit night I motored slowly home across the bay from Portland. A green, blinking, six-foot-tall metallic buoy marked the rocky point of House Island. To port, a red blinking buoy identified the edge of a mooring field extending off the shore of Peaks Island. Bobby Emerson's lobster boat was tied off there somewhere in the darkness. So was Dave Quinby's dive boat. I pulled back on the throttle, aware that late season lobster buoys were nearby.

The stars hung on the horizon, blending with the dark silhouette of Peaks Island and a cluster of lights on the wharf. I leaned forward against the windshield, concentrating. The glint of a half-submerged yellow buoy disappeared under the bow and thudded against the hull. I shifted the throttle into neutral. Too late; the line wrapped around the propeller and the engine came to a shuddering halt. I zipped up my life preserver. Lobsterman Bobby Emerson had warned me that it was only a matter of time before I picked up a trap at night. Everyone does. The longer a trap sits, the more weight on a buoy, until it settles beneath the surface. Bobby calls them ghost traps.

I tilted the engine up and, leaning over the stern, could see the rope wound around the prop in a tight loop. The buoy hung limply on the water. The propeller itself was undamaged. With a free hand I tried to unwind the rope but that went nowhere. I grabbed a serrated knife to cut the line. Then I remembered, Bobby hated the oversized stainless-steel props on pleasure boats that cut through his lines like butter. Inspecting my engine one day he said, "At least your dinky alloy prop gives my traps a decent chance. Remember that before you cut a line; it's someone's paycheck."

I grabbed a boat hook, thinking, if I haul the trap onboard, the pressure will release around the prop and I can release the line and the trap can settle to the bottom. What I was doing was technically illegal;

the fine for pulling another man's (or woman's) trap I'd heard was a gazillion dollars, but I put that aside and leaned into my work. Never mind that I was dressed in a dress shirt and tie; it felt good to use my back. In short order the deck was covered with slippery coils of line and clumps of rockweed and mud. I kicked the coils off to the side and regretted that I didn't have a pair of heavy work gloves. Instead of getting easier, the load increased as the trap neared the surface. Grabbing the edge of the trap I gave a grunt and barely lifted the trap to the rail. It was then that I noticed a second line running off the trap. No wonder the rig was so heavy, the lobsterman was fishing twins.

The whole mess started to slide overboard until I cleated off the second line. I abruptly realized that if I fell overboard, I wouldn't be able to climb back onboard. *Slow down. Slow down.* I glanced at the trap. It was packed with lobster and crab. From inside the cabin, I found a spare length of rope and tied one end around my waist and the other to the grab rail, just in case.

In another ten minutes, I was able to free the line from around the prop and released the trap into the water. Then I started the engine and pointed *SAKAMO* toward my mooring around the point. Tying off, I clambered into my dinghy and rowed to shore. Above the island, Orion rose higher in the sky.

By the time I reached our house I was shivering. My pants were torn below the knee, my windbreaker slick with engine grease, and my hair matted with mud. I recalled that when Sandi bought me the pants last month, she was proud that they were stain and rip resistant, to which I replied, "We'll see about that."

Tonight, she laughed and said she'd never seen me so attractive. Our counseling had gone well. I decided to stop my clinic on Chebeague Island after a family practice doctor, Patricia Phillips, was willing to add the clinic to her mainland practice in Yarmouth. It was a difficult decision but made easier when some of my favorite patients indicated they'd be willing to see me at my Portland office. I was trying, with some success, to simplify my life. Somehow, even with these changes, I was still working only a few hours less a week. Tonight was an omen. It was time to pull the boat. Maybe Saturday, if the wind stayed down.

On my way to clinic the following morning, I stopped at the Cockeyed Gull for coffee. Bobby Emerson motioned me over to his table and told me, in case I hadn't heard, that yesterday, the fireboat was called for Johnny Dinsmore, my favorite gout patient. Johnny had jacked his van up to replace a rusted muffler and the jack collapsed, pinning him underneath. If it hadn't been for a nearby neighbor who heard him groaning for help, he would have died. The police were there in minutes, the jack reset, and he was pulled out from beneath the van. Miraculously, he never lost consciousness. "Heard he broke a bunch of ribs," Bobby added. "In the emergency room, they put him on one of those breathing machines. His sister says a doctor Slocum is taking care of him in the ICU."

I made a note to see Johnny at the hospital. At his age, one complication often followed the next. He may have survived the accident, but would need good care and a bit of luck to avoid pneumonia.

Lois Herndon was my first patient of the day. After nearly a year on prednisone, I'd been able to taper her down to 3 milligrams, a dose she grudgingly admitted is a necessary evil. It was curious that at the onset of her vasculitis she required massive doses of steroids, but now only a few milligrams were necessary. She'd lost some of the weight the higher-dose steroids packed on, but her back was curved from the osteoporosis fracture she suffered last spring. I watched her limp through the door and grimace as she settled into a chair. *What now?*

Inside the exam room, she took off a shoe and rubbed her heel. She was worried about another stress fracture. I palpated the arch where it originated from the heel and she yelped. I placed a rigid arch inside her shoe and had her walk around the room. There was almost immediate improvement. The diagnosis: plantar fasciitis. Between regularly icing the heel, stretching, and naproxen, the heel pain would resolve.

An older man with metastatic prostate cancer to bone was next. A former rugby player, he'd lost sixty pounds, and loose skin draped off his upper arms in shapeless folds. The disease had spread despite radiation and hormonal treatment. I'd assumed his narcotic pain management from the oncologist—he could no longer tolerate the trip to town—and we had an honest conversation about end of life care. I thought back to the construction worker demanding narcotics for his bad back and moving like a young colt. The horrific outburst of cursing in the waiting room was worth the headache; word must have gotten out that I wasn't a soft touch.

My patient with prostate cancer was worried he was becoming addicted. I tried to explain to him that there was a big difference between taking morphine for bone cancer and patients with painful backs actively seeking out narcotics. He'd heard about my confrontation with the carpenter and smiled weakly that if he'd been there that day, he might have tripped the imposter on the way out. "Maybe then he'd know what real pain is about." I made a follow-up appointment for two weeks and asked if he'd heard much from his friends at the Lions Club. "They've been great. You were a member a few years back, weren't you?"

"I was. But that's before they sent back my renewal membership fee with a note, 'To be a Lion you must actually attend a meeting now and then.'"

We laughed. As he picked up his jacket to leave, his face drooped. "My wife Peggy is having a hard time, you know, with all of . . . you know, this. Maybe she should come by sometime soon and talk things over. I don't know if she might need some kind of pill."

"I'll be glad to see her. Anne can look on the schedule and give you an appointment on your way out." We shook hands and I watched him slowly shuffle out the door The tumor had spread to both kidneys. It wouldn't be long now.

Sister Mia was across the hall. Despite her best efforts, she'd slowly regained much of the weight she lost after her warning stroke, but to her credit, had stuck with her complex medication regimen for hypertension. I'd had to add back some insulin to control her blood sugars and increase the dose of her cholesterol lowering medication. "Sister Mia," I began, "I haven't seen you out walking with the other sisters. And your weight, you were doing such a great job of—"

Sister Mia visibly stiffened and pulled at the edge of her habit. "Well then, if I may ask, when was the last time you ran around the island? I used to see you regularly moving along at a good clip without a care in the world. Now the only time I see you run is when you're late for the ferry. I think seeing you run did more to get me out walking than any lecture. What happened?"

What happened? Life happened, I thought. Two children, a stressful job with unpredictable hours, not enough time, that's what happened. "I'm running," I lied, though technically that was true. As she said, I often ran to catch the ferry. "You just don't always see me. In fact, I was just thinking of getting out over lunch for a quick run."

As a former parochial school teacher, Sister Mia could root out a fib like a lie detector. "Then of course you have brought your running shorts to clinic today?"

I rubbed my forehead. "Okay," I admitted, "I don't have my running shorts. But I'm thinking about running. I just might go home and change and get out for a run."

Sister Mia leaned forward. "You are a dear man, Dr. Radis. I suggest you take the time to go home, change, and go out for a run. Now, get going."

After Sister Mia's visit, Anne informed me that my last two patients of the morning had rescheduled. I took that as a sign. I biked home and changed and hit the road. The first mile I was winded. I slowed and turned onto a narrow winding dirt path and expected my breathing to slow. When it didn't, I stopped and walked. The trail followed a meandering brook. I watched a dozen deer graze peacefully among the rose hips and beach peas. A mound of brush and branches sat squarely in the middle of the stream. It was a beaver lodge. Not far downstream, I found a newly constructed dam and fresh tracks in the mud. I felt more relaxed than I had in months.

Returning to the road along the back shore of Peaks, I broke into a run again, but felt flat. I wasn't getting my expected second wind. And was that a faint, aching pressure in my chest? By the time I arrived home, I was concerned. My chest symptoms resolved, but I knew something wasn't right. I felt okay, but not great. What would I say if a patient of mine described a similar history? My mind raced forward and backward. What if I wasn't merely out of shape? My dad was 43 at the time of his fatal heart attack. His sister suffered her first heart attack at 38. At 37, I was young, yes, but a candidate for heart disease nevertheless.

I was alone in the house; Kate was in school, Molly at daycare, Sandi at work. I was eleven again, walking home from the school playground where my oldest brother Rick met me and sat me down and told me that tonight dad had a problem with his heart. We sat for a few minutes, then he said, "I think he died." Neither one of us knew how to cry.

After taking an aspirin, I called for an appointment with my doctor, internist Dan Merson. He returned my call as I was getting out of the shower, and after hearing my story, decided to fit me in the same afternoon for a treadmill rather than sending me to the emergency room. I arrived early, and joked with the male nurse as he shaved portions of my chest to attach the electrical leads. Then Dr. Merson initiated a Bruce protocol; a progressive change in both speed and elevation at three-minute intervals. By now, I'd convinced myself that I was over-reacting, that Sister Mia had done me a favor by getting me back on the road to fitness and everything was going to be fine. Ever the competitor, I prepped myself to push hard.

I walked slowly the first three minutes, and broke into a slow, effortless jog as the treadmill speed and incline increased. Then, at an effort I might make jogging up a single flight of stairs, Dr. Merson signaled to the tech it was time to stop. I wasn't even breathing hard. Dan silently studied the readout at length before passing me the strip. At a glance, it was clear why he'd discontinued the test. The EKG readout demonstrated the typical findings of ischemic heart disease: horizontal and down-sloping ST segment depression.

Dan had me take a seat and, encouragingly, took a less than definitive approach to the results of my treadmill. "Chuck, I'm going to ask Charlie Hoag in cardiology to repeat the treadmill. Even with these kinds of changes it's possible this is a false positive. You may have normal coronary arteries, but then again maybe you don't, and maybe this a stroke of luck, diagnosing this before you suffer a heart attack. You okay?"

Head down, I was still studying the readout in disbelief. "This is my EKG?"

"Chuck, let's take it one step at a time. Dr. Hoag's office will contact you." He handed me a cup of water. "I want you to take one baby aspirin daily. And no running for now. Not until Hoag says it's okay. Oh, one more thing, I'm calling in a prescription for sublingual nitroglycerin if the chest symptoms recur. I want you to promise me you'll take the fireboat in if the nitroglycerin doesn't resolve your symptoms.

On my way to the hospital for rounds, I felt my pulse; it was slow and regular. My blood pressure at Dr. Merson's office was normal. My cholesterol from my physical six months ago was excellent. Get a grip, I told myself, follow your doctor's advice, and accept wherever the diagnosis leads.

Right now, my job was to see Johnny Dinsmore. In the ICU, Dr. Slocum was gowned and gloved at his bedside. He looked up briefly in recognition before advancing a needle through Johnny's chest wall. The syringe filled with muddy, partially clotted blood. Then he advanced a catheter over the needle into the space between the lungs and fractured ribs and hooked the unit to a negative pressure drainage bag on the bed rail. I leaned in for a closer look. Johnny's nose looked dislocated and bruises extended below his eyes to his upper lip. Although he was heavily sedated, and his face partially obscured by the taped endotracheal tube, I swore he was smiling.

I followed Dr. Slocum out to the nursing station. "He's one of your patient's on Peaks, isn't he? Poor guy, he has a flail chest; the upper four ribs on both sides of the sternum are fractured. To be truthful, I didn't think he was going to make it out of the ER. Every time he gasped for breath his ribs collapsed inward. I had to intubate him ten minutes after he arrived. We had to transfuse him with six units of blood and he's still oozing blood into his chest. But look at his heart rate and blood pressure. They're like a rock. I mean does this guy feel pain?"

I thought back to Johnny's grand indifference to gout, a disease that some say is the male equivalent to childbirth. "No," I said. He's a different kind of cat."

Slocum swiveled in his chair. Some vague instinct tugged at him and he asked, "Are you okay?"

"Good. I feel fine. Even had time for a quick run today."

Dr. Slocum gave me a curious look, but returned to his dictation when I didn't volunteer more. A few minutes later I was out the door and headed for the second floor to continue rounds.

That night, as we showered together, Sandi showed no surprise as I recounted the events of the day. Only minutes before she'd believed her husband was in mint condition, and now I was telling her that my coronary arteries might be partially blocked. She took in the uncertainty and asked a few questions. I didn't have the answers. Then she took my hand and pronounced with absolute conviction, "I think you're going to be just fine." That night, she drifted off a moment after her head hit the pillow. When I arose at one a.m. unable to sleep, she was still lightly humming.

Charlie Hoag, the cardiologist, phoned early the next morning, a Saturday, and wanted to talk. His questions were more probing and direct than Dan Merson's. From the rustling paper in the background, I suspected he was reviewing my treadmill EKG. "So, how far into your island run were you when you developed symptoms?"

"Maybe a couple of miles." I said.

"And how fast were you going?"

"I'm not sure, maybe a seven-minute mile pace, maybe a little faster.

There was a pause on the other end. "That's pretty quick. Your EKG tracing I'm reviewing looks like it became abnormal at no more than a slow jog."

"I know. Dan had me stop before I even got going. I felt fine."

"Listen, tell you what, why don't you drop by bright and early Monday morning and we'll get an echocardiogram and following that, I'll repeat the treadmill. This time I'll really push you, and at your absolute peak heart rate, I'll inject thallium into your IV and we'll get a better sense of your heart function. Oh, and one more thing, you *did* fill the sublingual prescription for nitroglycerin Dan Merson called in?" Evidently, Dr. Hoag didn't fully trust me, which I was fine with. If I were him, I wouldn't trust me either. Doctors are notoriously bad patients.

"I've got it right here on the bed stand."

"Good. If you need to use it, call for the fireboat and I'll meet you in the ER."

Two days later, I was hooked up for another treadmill. Off to the side I noticed an emergency crash cart with a defibrillator unit. A radiology tech stood by with a vial of radioactive thallium to inject at peak exercise. Two medical students hovered in the background. Dr. Hoag started the treadmill and I shuffled along for three minutes. At the point when Dr. Merson shut down the test, I broke into a slow jog for three

DR. CHARLES RADIS   151

minutes, then an easy run, before changing gears into a steady run. "Let me know if you're having any chest pain." Charlie said, studying the EKG readouts.

I nodded and concentrated on running an all-out effort. My calves were burning and I gasped for breath as the treadmill speed and incline increased. Finally, I gave a signal, and the treadmill stopped. The tech laid me down, injected the thallium, and scanned my heart. I was winded, but the chest aching I'd experienced on my run around the island never recurred. The effort left me drained but at least I'd established for myself that I could push myself hard and not worry about . . . well . . . dropping dead. It happens.

I accepted a towel and a drink of water. On the screen I could see my heart rate slowly drifting down. Dr. Hoag took a chair next to me and organized the readouts. I finished the glass of water. "Thanks for letting me go all-out." I said. "I couldn't have gone on much longer before collapsing."

Charlie reviewed the thallium scan images closely. "Chuck, you did very well. I don't get to do treadmills very often on former college runners, but your scan was very disturbing. The ultrasound shows that the bottom portion of your heart doesn't contract normally and the EKG shows the same deep ST segment abnormalities you had on Dr Merson's treadmill. I can either start you on a long-term beta blocker, a statin, and continue the twice daily nitroglycerin, or . . . " He paused so that I could absorb the full impact of what he was saying. ". . . I can schedule you for a cardiac catheterization. We still don't have a good understanding of your vascular anatomy."

"Seriously?"

"Chuck. I'm a cardiologist. This is your heart."

I didn't hesitate. My breathing was back to normal. My head was clear. He had my full attention. "I'll go for the catheterization."

"Good. That's what I'd recommend. I'll get it set up. We'll hold off on the other meds for now, except the aspirin and twice daily nitroglycerin."

The next few days were remarkably worry free. It helped that Sandi remained convinced that I was basically healthy. As a plumber's assistant she'd seen her share of plugged-up pipes respond to skilled interventions. In her mind, an angiogram made perfect sense. If there was a narrowed artery, the angiographer could insert a stent or inflate a balloon to expand the vessel. What's more, whatever was behind my abnormal studies, it hadn't prevented me from running deep into the treadmill protocol. She remained optimistic. On the night before the angiogram, the hospital scheduler called and informed me that instead of an 11:00 a.m. procedure, I was bumped up to the first case at 7:00 a.m. That meant arriving at the hospital before 6:00.

Anxious to have the study done, I said yes. Okay, that complicated things. The first morning ferry from Peaks to Portland departed at 6:15. That meant I'd take *SAKAMO* to Portland in the dark. I checked the marine radio report. Wind speeds were predicted at less than five knots. Skies were clear. No fog in the extended forecast. In my pocket calendar I wrote: *Stay in shipping channel. Pay attention. Avoid lobster buoys.*

There was one problem, the change in time meant I'd have to go in alone. Sandi would come in on a later ferry after she dropped Kate off at school and Molly at a friend's house. What if something went wrong during the procedure? I knew from several of my own patients that complications during angiograms, though infrequent, could be serious. These include, but are not limited to, cardiac arrhythmia, stroke, myocardial infarction, arterial dissection, and, of course, death.

I awoke at 4:45 and quietly dressed. I kissed both Kate and Molly goodbye; it would have been bad luck if I hadn't. Sandi repeated that everything was going to be fine and that she'd see me in a few hours. We acted as if it were commonplace to kiss your husband goodbye and watch him go by boat to a cardiac catheterization. Then I walked down to the beach, put on my life preserver, and dragged the dinghy to the waterline. A late-setting waxing moon lingered over Portland's skyline. Underway, a graceful V extended behind *SAKAMO*. Behind me, the faint glow of another sunrise softened the eastern horizon.

Preparations for the angiogram gave me little time for second thoughts. I signed the permit and was immediately wheeled into the procedure suite, where a tech scrubbed my right groin where the catheter would be inserted into the femoral artery. The anesthesiologist placed an IV in my forearm, and then, lights out. I'm a lightweight when it comes to sedation.

When I awoke in the recovery room, a nurse was applying pressure to my groin to ensure that I didn't bleed excessively from the arterial puncture. That's when Sandi walked in. As the nurse hovered over my groin, she informed Sandi that the procedure had gone well and that the doctor would be in shortly. Sandi asked if it was okay if she took over. She didn't like the idea of a pretty nurse casually pressuring my groin. The nurse said no. Sandi came over to the bed and ran a hand through my hair and impulsively gave me a kiss.

Charlie Hoag came through the door and was beaming. It's not often a cardiologist can deliver good news. "Chuck, your coronary arteries are in perfect shape. We did confirm that the inferior aspect of your left ventricle doesn't contract normally. I think that's what accounts for your abnormal scan and treadmill. Sometimes a viral infection can affect the heart; it could have happened in childhood or it could have been last year. That drags down your ejection range to the lower limit of normal. The important thing is that the remainder of your heart pumps like a champ."

"Do I need to take medications?"

"No medications."

"Running?"

"You're good to go."

A few hours later, after lunch at Becky's on the waterfront, Sandi and I cruised back to the island. Whitecaps rolled in from the north. A line of double-crested cormorants winged southward, their wingtips skimming the tops of the waves. I thought of my father, Frank G Radis, and wondered if he'd had any warning signs before his fatal heart attack. He never had a second chance. Most of us don't.

That night, I called several of my high-school friends to chat. Over the years, except for our yearly winter camping trips, I'd drifted away from regular contact. It's easy to make excuses that you don't have time to maintain friendships when life gets busy. My marriage wasn't the only thing I needed to nurture. Being a good doctor isn't simply about being the best diagnostician, it's about being your best self. I needed to remember that.

A few days later, I bought my first treadmill, trucked it over on the car ferry, and set it up next to my desk, facing the bay. With winter close by, I couldn't let a little wind and snow slow me down.

17

I t was New Year's Eve on Peaks Island. A slushy mixture of ice and seawater churned and ground against the beach. A pale-yellow half-moon threw a faint shadow over the schoolyard. Sandi and I leaned into the wind as we inched our way uphill, barely at eye level with plowed snow.

A dug path led to a modest shed-roofed cottage. Opening the door, our neighbor Arnold Berndt, bent-backed and mostly deaf, extended a hand and welcomed us inside. "It's not much," he said, loud enough for him to hear himself, "but it keeps the rain out!" Arnold's son, Peter—who undoubtedly shoveled the pathway—took our coats and offered us a glass of wine. Across from where we sat, a chestnut-stained bookshelf took up an entire wall. High up on the bookcase, an ancient copper lamp hung from a chain next to the books. Arnold settled into a recliner and folded his hands, silently tapping his index fingers together.

As he shifted his head, he suddenly yelped and reached back to rub his neck. The sound was involuntary and sharp, like a wounded animal, and I realized his pain must be from the neuralgia I was treating him for. Though Arnold had been my patient for several years, I knew little about him beyond that he was born and raised in Germany and that he'd recently lost his wife of more than fifty years, Erna. He spent much of his day and night in the back room, resting in bed. Even as I'd titrated the dose higher and higher, the gabapentin I'd prescribed for the nerve pain had been ineffective. Luckily, his son Peter was visiting from Europe and could shop and cook. As Mr. Berndt had declined, several island neighbors now stopped by regularly with hot meals and kept him informed of island news.

"You know," Arnold said, in a thick German accent, "I heard Hitler speak." A blast of wind funneled up from the beach through a grove of staghorn sumac and alders, rattling and groaning against the cottage, the cottage that Arnold and Erna built by hand a few years after they first visited Peaks Island in the 1960s. I leaned forward. Arnold's voice dropped to a whisper. "I went to a rally in . . . 1933. Yes, in 1933. Hitler's voice was like both honey and hissing acid. He was not yet in power, but you could see it coming. I remember looking round at my friends and neighbors. They were nodding their heads in agreement.

"Hitler's power grew. He was a madman, yes, but he was patient and understood and played on the common man's prejudices. The next year I gathered my belongings and slipped out of Germany illegally; I was of draft age. Everywhere I traveled, I was viewed with suspicion. I was not Jewish but an unwelcome German refugee."

Arnold's eyes widened, unblinking. He took a sip of wine and swallowed. Even the simple act of swallowing seemed to aggravate his pain. He reached up and massaged his neck. I thought back to my first glimpse of Arnold as he'd skimmed across the bay windsurfing. When he pulled up on the beach, I walked over to chat and was taken aback that I was meeting a wisp of an old man with just enough muscle tone to lug the sailboard above the high-tide mark. I told him that I worried that if he slipped off the board, he lacked the strength to save himself. But Arnold was deceptive. His strength, he told me, was in his balance and feel for the wind. He never fell. It seemed beyond belief that he taught sailing at Trefethen, our local boating club.

"As Hitler consolidated his power, Europe looked the other way," Arnold continued, his voice growing stronger. "I kept on the move. I met Erna, my future wife, in Italy. She was the daughter of a Catholic mother and an absent Jewish father; her goal was to reach Palestine. We formed a strong bond, but money? We had barely enough to board a freighter for Palestine. It was said that in Palestine, we could sit out the coming war. On the fourth night at sea, I was on deck watching for the coast. Ahead I could see lights. It was Palestine. Then I heard voices up on the bow. The crew was ordered to turn the ship around. The port was closed to us.

"I found Erna. 'Come. Leave our belongings. Take what you can carry. We need to go.' The freighter began a slow turn, and we stood on the rail and jumped. We swam toward shore. Somehow, we made the beach and were found the next morning."

"Did they allow you to stay?" I asked.

"Yes, but I was initially interned by the British authorities because of my German nationality. Erna found work as a nanny for the district commissioner of Jerusalem. We married within the year."

"That's an amazing story," I said. "Thank you."

We sat quietly, alone in our thoughts. Outside, the snow continued to blow. Peter poured his father and me another glass of wine. Sandi pointed to a wood-framed photo on the bookcase and asked Mr. Berndt, "Is that Erna and you in Palestine?"

Without looking up, Mr. Berndt said, "Yes. That was taken the day Erna was promoted. She became the district commissioner's secretary. It came with a small raise. They recognized that she was an educated woman, a competent woman. We were happy."

I looked over to Sandi. It was time to go, but Mr. Berndt raised a hand. "Please stay." He cautiously swallowed another sip of wine, exhaled, and relaxed against the headrest. We waited.

"My wife and I lived in Palestine from 1934 to 1948. The Jews were sent to concentration camps in Europe, but in Palestine, they themselves persecuted the Arabs. Two wrongs do not make a right. Always, we see our differences more than our similarities. Even here, on Peaks Island, because I am German and I speak with an accent, they assume certain things. It has not always been easy.

"Let me tell you a story. One day in Palestine, two Christian priests visited the consulate. They were of different denominations. They requested a meeting with the head man, the district commissioner. He invited them in; Erna served tea. The two men sat across from the commissioner in their gold and scarlet robes. The shorter of the two held a cardboard box. He explained that their congregations shared an ancient stone church of worship in Jerusalem. Although both congregations claimed ownership of the church, a compromise was working, a schedule rigidly adhered to. At certain times, on certain days, one congregation came to worship. On other days, at certain times, it was the other congregation's turn. The two congregations rarely saw each other. It was better that way."

"The taller priest took up the story, 'On the ceiling and walls of our church are dozens and dozens of hanging lamps, some, it's said, dating back to the time of Christ. The lamps are revered. Each congregation understands which lamps belong to whom, their ownership traced back through generations of worshippers. And on this,' he turned to the shorter priest who listened attentively, 'there is general agreement.'

"The British commissioner said to the two men, 'Well, I must say, I congratulate you. The memories of Arabs, Christians, and Jews are long. We must spread this spirit you have found in your hearts.'

"The two holy men's eyes fell toward their laps. They fiddled with their ornamentation. Then one of the priests gently opened the box. Erna placed a tray of pastry on the table between the priests and the commissioner. She lingered by the door, listening, and watching. A dented, smoke-stained copper hanging lamp was removed from the box. The two priests held the lamp in tandem, each maintaining a grip, and placed it on the table. The lamp looked like it could be fifty years old or more than a thousand. Who could say?

"'We agree on the ownership for each lamp,' the taller of the two priests said. 'All of them, except for this one. This special lamp, by our records, clearly belongs to us. It has belonged to us for more than 500 years, perhaps longer.'

"'By our records,' the shorter priest interrupted, his voice rising, 'This lamp belongs to our congregation. It is sacred to our people. We had no idea the other congregation claimed this lamp as their own until very recently. We have come to you for a solution. You must decide. There are those in my congregation who feel that the only solution is to take what is ours.' Then he removed a sheath of yellowed papers from his satchel and declared, 'Here is our proof of ownership for the lamp.'

"'And here is proof of our ownership,' The taller priest replied quickly, removing an envelope from beneath his vestments. In fact—' but the commissioner waved him off and motioned for Erna.

"The priests settled back into their chairs, eyeing each other suspiciously. Erna refilled their teacups. The British commissioner rested his hand on his chin before awkwardly crossing and re-crossing his arms. He silently noted that the two men were not armed. Good. Then he slowly reached out and picked up the lamp and turned it from side to side, studying it from all angles.

"'Erna,' he said finally, 'Place these documents in my briefcase by the door. Then lock the clasp. I have the key.' Then he turned to the priests and said, 'I can see how critical it is to determine the true owner-ship of this sacred lamp. Of course, I don't have the expertise to make this decision, but we have experts in Great Britain, world-renowned experts, who can properly determine the true ownership of the lamp. Now that you have provided me with the evidence and the lamp, I believe we have everything we need to make a decision.'

"He stood and shook each of the priest's hands. 'Will you each abide by my decision?' The two holy men agreed, each believing that the experts would surely conclude the righteousness of their case. 'Good. With your permission,' the commissioner continued, 'I will take this lamp and send it on to Great Britain by steamer. There's no question we can properly get to the bottom of this.'

"The Priests seemed relieved to have a third party, a world-renowned expert, settle the question. The solution seemed perfectly rea-sonable. 'Of course, it may take time,' the commissioner added. 'There's a war going on, you know.' The priests said they understood. In another moment, they were gone.

"Erna cleared the table. The commissioner picked up the ancient lamp and held the door for her. 'My Dear Erna, I have one more item for you.' He gently placed the lamp on the tray and picking up a nap-kin, dabbed his mouth and wiped his hands. 'Take this lamp. Promise me that I will never see it again. Do you understand? Never.'"

In the silence that followed, Mr. Berndt's hands settled on his lap, his eyes alert and bright. Peter quietly cleared off the table. Sandi and I zipped up our parkas. "The lamp," Mr. Berndt's eyes rested on me. His weariness was gone, and the edges of his mouth curled upward in a curi-ous smile. "You can take a look at the lamp if you wish." He pointed toward the top corner of the bookcase. There, in a musty corner, hang-ing from a chain, was the disputed lamp.

Several nights later, I returned from a house call and waved my tooth-brush under the faucet. Nothing. Hearing me mutter a few foul words, Sandi joined me in the bathroom and was shocked that her latest repairs with her plumber boss Paul, had failed to prevent a freeze-up.

She checked the heat tape. It was plugged in. We unscrewed the panel behind the pipes and inspected the fiberglass insulation. It was stapled in place. The basic, immutable problem was that our bathroom was on the windward, outside wall of the house. When it dropped below zero and the wind blew, our pipes froze.

On the other hand, there was something close to romantic about defrosting pipes with your spouse. Sandi sat cross-legged on the linoleum in her pink bathrobe aiming her hairdryer at a spot where a pipe disappeared under the sink into the subfloor. I pointed my hairdryer where another pipe took a 90-degree twist. The portable heating hummed directly below us in the downstairs bathroom.

Sandi said, "I was talking to Dan Durgin about our cemetery plots today."

"No kidding." I looked up from my work. "What was it, last summer I asked him if there was room for us in Pond Grove cemetery? What did he say today?"

"He said they're working on it."

"That's encouraging. When I didn't hear back, I wondered if there was some special list, invitation only, to qualify for a spot. Was he friendly?" I wondered.

"Definitely. Paul and I put in a new sink for him a few weeks ago. He and his wife have a lovely house."

That's the thing about Sandi, she knew everyone on the island, and what's more, she was on good terms with most of them. It was unusual for a woman to be a plumber, but we lived in a community of quirky, unusual people, and Sandi fit right in. A rattling sound echoed from the pipe. Sandi turned off her hairdryer and listened. "We've got some movement." Moments later a glassy drop released into the sink followed by a slushy mix of freezing tap water. "Let's keep the hot water running for another fifteen minutes," Sandi cautioned. "Then I'll set it to a slow drip. Oh, do you remember, tomorrow is Saturday. You promised to be with Kate and Molly while I take the 8:15 morning ferry to town for a piano lesson."

"Of course," I said, opening my pocket calendar, and rediscovering the reminder. "The children can accompany me on a house call in the morning. Kate is an old hand at house calls, and she'll have Molly to supervise. I'll pack a couple of coloring books and snacks. It should be fun."

At sunrise, I filled the upstairs bathroom sink with hot water to shave while Sandi showered. In a few minutes, Kate came stumbling in holding one edge of her favorite blanket and peed in the toilet. Molly followed Kate in and stood quietly in her diaper next to her sister with a binky in her mouth. After shaving, I dressed quickly in our bedroom, eyeing the clock, and hurried downstairs, poured cereal into bowls, and placed two prunes on the edge of Molly's plate; a nod to Sandi's concerns regarding constipation in our two-year-old. Coffee pot on, good. Bread in the toaster. Done.

There was a countdown in our household for making the ferry. It was critical we headed out in the truck no later than 8:06 to make the 8:15 ferry. To improve our chances, we set the clock five minutes ahead and pretended it was the true time. With this mindset, even with the inevitable missing boot or mitten, it was rare that we missed a ferry.

Sandi was not the wildcard, nor was Molly, she was at an age where she still passively accepted help with her snowsuit and boots. It was the two knuckleheads, Kate and me, who invariably couldn't connect with some vital piece of outerwear as we headed out the door into the cold. Fortunately, Sandi had packed Kate and Molly's backpacks last night and hung them by the outside door. After breakfast, as I cleared the table, she rode herd on Kate, while I folded Molly into her snowsuit.

I glanced at the clock. Fantastic. We had one full minute. At my desk, I grabbed my satchel and made sure it contained my stethoscope, blood pressure cuff, and blood draw kit. Anything else? I decided to bring my black bag filled with my what-ifs, as in, what if I needed to dress a wound? Did I have specimen cups for cultures? Did I have an additional light source? There was no way to anticipate everything. Luckily, I was not traveling to another island; if I needed something, I could always open the health center. Today, I was looking forward to visiting Ruth, my patient with chronic schizophrenia. After several visits to the health center, her paranoia had returned, and she preferred the familiarity and isolation of her cottage.

By the time I scurried up the wooden walkway, Sandi was in the driver's seat, the children buckled up in the back. And instead of a look of exasperation, she smiled sweetly at me; before breakfast I had turned on the truck defroster. Instead of peering through an opening clear of ice the size of a postage stamp, the windshield was completely defrosted. We parked in front of the post office and Sandi made the 8:15 ferry by a full three minutes.

Scenes like ours were the rule for island families where one or both parents worked in town, and the reason why so many moved off after a year or two. The cumulative frustration of dealing with the ferry schedule eventually outweighed any romantic notions about island life. At Lisa's café, I sat with a cup of coffee while Kate and Molly snacked on a bagel and cream cheese. Bobby Emerson was almost out the door before he saw me and circled back. "Hear about Rick Crowley?" He dropped his voice. "Bad accident out scalloping yesterday. You know that old hydraulic drum he operates at midship to control the cable to his dragger? He was out by House Island with his wife, Nancy, when a finger of his work glove got caught in the drum."

Bobby glanced down at Kate and Molly who'd taken out their coloring books and motioned for me to join him at another table. "Ricky yanked back on the glove but by then, with the drum spinning, his entire hand was buried in cable, and the drum spun the hand around and around. His whole body rotated and twisted up in the air. All this time, he's screaming for Nancy to cut the emergency power. She stopped the drum and put it in neutral and was able to back off the cable pinning Ricky's hand. The hand wasn't severed but stretched out like nobody's business. It flopped toward the deck like a piece of rubber. Ricky cradled it with his other hand and Nancy put out a distress call. Luckily, the Coast Guard was nearby, and they were able to transfer him to town where an ambulance rushed him to Maine Medical Center."

"Did they amputate the hand?" I asked.

"From what I heard, some hot shot hand surgeon happened to be in the ER finishing up another case and they whisked Ricky upstairs to the operating room. Ricky called me this morning. He's doped up but managed to talk. Every tendon at his elbow was ripped clear off. His nerves were stretched, the muscles in his hand were like mush. It took more than six hours for the surgeon to reattach everything. It's anyone's guess what use he'll have of that hand."

There was a brief silence between us. I couldn't imagine completely losing the use of my dominant hand. With the improvements in prosthesis in recent years, I wondered if Rick would have been better off if they'd removed the hand. Bobby leaned in. "Speaking of accidents waiting to happen, I've watched you row out to your boat a few times."

"Am I doing something wrong?" I asked.

"No, and I'm glad you're wearing a life-preserver."

"So, what's your point? I've done it a hundred times now, and I've got a good routine."

"A mooring is no place to keep a commuter boat this time of year. When you slip getting into your dinghy, you're a good fifty yards offshore in freezing water, weighed down by your clothes, and maybe panicking that you can't keep your head above water. I'm not saying if, I'm saying *when* you fall in."

"What are you getting at, that I get rid of my boat?" I was getting defensive. "Just because I didn't grow up around the water doesn't mean I'm incompetent." I was fuming.

"Nothing like that. *SAKAMO* is a solid little boat." Bobby stretched out his legs and drained the last of his coffee. "For now, if you want, tie up on my float on the back edge of the Army pier. Coming down a ladder to your boat is a whole lot safer than rowing a dinghy in the dark. Better yet, tie up *SAKAMO* in Portland for the next few months and rely on the ferry. Come spring, I'll help you build a float. We'll tow it over to the Army pier and chain it to the wharf. If we do that, let's build the float long enough so that Rick Crowley can use it for his dinghy. Things look bad for him now, but he'll be back."

I helped the girls back into their parkas and thanked Bobby. Of course, he was right.

After our second breakfast, I turned the truck around, drove up a rutted dirt road across from Feeney's Market, and parked beneath a towering white pine. I held Molly in one arm as Kate followed in my boot steps through the crusty, foot-deep snow. Ruth knew we were coming, but just because she agreed to a house call yesterday, didn't mean she was in the mood today. I rapped on the door.

Ruth pulled back the curtain at the window and stared for a long moment. Then she disappeared and cracked open the door. "What are their names? The children, what are their names?"

I stepped forward, still holding Molly. "This is Molly, she's nearly three, and behind me is Kate, age six."

The door swung open and the odor of stale cigarette smoke met us. I looked over to the bed against the far wall and spied an ashtray on the bedstand with a mound of cigarette butts spilling over the edges. Ruth held an unlit cigarette in her yellowed fingers and quietly dropped it into the sink. "Well, well, two children, that's good, that's very good." We stood awkwardly for a moment before Kate spied several windup toys on the bookshelf and picked one up.

"When you wind up the kangaroo, it moves forward on these little wheels," Ruth explained as she gently took the toy from Kate's hand and showed her how to wind it up. Then she bent down to the floor with surprising agility and released the pocket-sized kangaroo. It moved steadily across the uneven wooden floor until it abruptly flipped and landed on its feet. Kate squealed with delight and Molly wiggled out of my arms to join her sister.

I sat on the edge of the bed next to Ruth and placed my stethoscope on her chest. Her tiny dog, Lisa, peeked out from the edge of the bedsheets. No use to show herself with two unpredictable children in the cottage. The lung sounds were a cacophony of high-pitched wheezes and groans. I asked her if she was coughing, and in response she hacked up a plug of creamy gelatinous phlegm. The relatively normal-colored phlegm was the best evidence that she was not actively infected and that this was an exacerbation of her emphysema. I wondered if she'd accept an inhaler?

"Ruth, about the cigarettes. It would be fantastic if you could quit, but short of that, can you cut back?"

Without answering, Ruth pulled down her stocking to reveal a ragged cut across her shin. There was no Band-Aid or antiseptic on the wound. The edges gaped open and pus dripped down the front of her shin. "I tore it on the edge of the bed last week. Right there." She pointed to the metal frame of the bed.

I ran a finger over the sharp corner, nearly slicing my finger. Okay, things were piling up here fast. This was supposed to be a simple follow-up. "Do you have some tape?" I asked. Ruth pointed to a drawer. Inside, was a roll of packing tape and nestled next to it, a vial of Thorazine. Perfect; this was like a treasure hunt. I'd been wondering where she kept her prescription bottles. But first, I grabbed a loose sock from the floor and taped it around the metal corner. I opened up my backpack and found an inhaler.

Handing it to her, she tore open the box excitedly, as if it were a Christmas present. "Oh, this will work fine. We remember this. I've used this before; it's very good!"

I cleaned the wound with Betadine and applied a sterile dressing. Normally, an infection like this should heal with good local care, but this was not normally. I picked up the phone and called in an antibiotic prescription to Rosemont Pharmacy in Portland. If all went well, the prescription should arrive off the 2:15 ferry and one of the crew could bring it up the hill to Feeney's Market. From there, Heather, the cashier, might drop the prescription off on her way home tonight. That was a lot of mights and shoulds. I pulled out my pocket calendar and wrote: *Call Ruth Monday. Make sure she has antibiotic.* As an afterthought I wrote: *Needs pneumonia vaccine.*

Gathering up Kate and Molly, I zipped up their jackets. Ruth gifted Kate the wind-up kangaroo. In the palm of Molly's hand, she placed a plastic pink pig. We stepped outside and picked our way back to the truck, backtracking through our frozen footprints. Against the trunk of the white pine I clicked my boots together to remove a clump of ice and noticed a line of creamy whitewash on the trunk. Several pellets embedded with tiny bones and fur lay on the top of the snow. I looked up. A great horned owl was perched on a low branch eyeing me with disinterest.

I whispered to Kate and Molly, "Look up." Kate gazed silently upward before squatting down and pointed out the owl to Molly, who clapped her hands in excitement. The owl silently spread its wings and flew across the road, deeper into the woods.

18

A week later, the temperature plummeted to minus eight degrees and the hydraulics controlling the transfer bridge on the Peaks Island wharf froze solid on an outgoing tide. Over a hundred islanders, a third of them middle- and high-school students, huddled on the wharf waiting to board the 7:15 ferry to the mainland. The crew cleated off the bow six feet below the lip, and a deckhand clambered up a ladder onto the transfer bridge, where he whacked the hydraulic mechanism with a wrench. This "repair" was unsuccessful.

Captain Hogan climbed out of the pilot house and strolled out to the bow. He pointed to a pile of wooden pallets and instructed the crew to stack four of them on the deck close to the bow, and pointed to where a smaller stack of two pallets should be placed. Then he ordered the crew to lift a gangplank to the apron of the transfer bridge, tie it off, and snug up the other end to the highest pallet. In another ten minutes, a line of gangplanks formed a smooth, continuous drop to the deck.

The captain walked the plank, leaning against the hand rails here and there, trying to see if a simple shift in weight would cause the ramp to come tumbling down. Satisfied, he motioned for the passengers (including Sandi) to board. In groups of five, passengers shuffled uncertainly onto the catwalk. Sandi thought this was great fun. An elderly neighbor of ours inched forward, both hands gripping the icy rails of the gangplank. She noticed Sandi and gave a sweet wave. Sandi yelled, "You go girl!"

Paul Erico was called to the Peaks Island Inn to assess the damage from a burst pipe in the second-floor bathroom. The water had run undetected over the weekend until it collapsed the downstairs ceiling. My first patient at the health center, already aware that the Inn was closed until further notice, declared the inn "a Jonah," an archaic term for bad luck.

The recent construction of the upscale inn was viewed, by some, as a harbinger of the future, a future of wealthy summer people transforming Peaks Island from a year-round community into a summer colony. Tourists have frequented Peaks for more than a hundred years, but until recently the balance between year-rounders and summer visitors favored the needs and concerns of islanders. That was slowly changing.

From the start, the inn was controversial. Built at the site of a former gas station, the contaminated soil from the underground tanks was not properly disposed of off-island. Instead of rental rooms, there were suites with names like the Jewell Island suite and the Ram Island suite. On the ground floor was a restaurant and bar and a banquet room for weddings along with an outdoor seasonal tent with a view of the bay. This would all be standard fare for, say Cape Cod, but for Peaks Island the scale of the building set tongues clicking.

Island historian William Jordan articulated the concerns of some islanders when he publicly weighed in on both the inn and the owner's new home on the back shore. "This lady may be able to build herself a 4,000 square foot starter castle, but she'll always need the natives to carry her cases of champagne and caviar."

But it wasn't only the inn triggering concerns. With rising house prices (even uninsulated, seasonal cottages a half-mile from the water were selling for twice what they did ten years before) and upcoming island property revaluations, many islanders feared they would be taxed out of their homes. Long Island, another Portland city island, had already laid down the gauntlet; they'd voted to secede from Portland and incorporate as Maine's newest town. An active group on Peaks was exploring secession as well.

Bundled up on a recent run last week, I almost missed a new sign on the telephone pole down by Pumpkin Knob: *Keep Off Beach: Private Property*. A few days later, the sign was mysteriously torn down, but almost immediately another sign, higher up on the telephone pole, replaced it. In fairness, according to Maine law, homeowners own the beach down to low-tide mark, but in practice, no one ever cared if islanders sunbathed, walked, or picnicked on the beaches. Now that most of the waterfront properties on Peaks had been sold to seasonal residents, it was inevitable that there would be more conflict.

At the door to the health center, I broke off a two-foot ice stalactite hanging from the eave and stomped my feet in the foyer before entering the waiting room. The Quinby children, Kipp, Trent, and Dale, were on the carpet playing with Legos. I stopped for a moment to chat with Dave about the frozen transfer bridge. The wind, more than the frigid temperatures, had kept him off the water today. He unzipped his parka. "Once I'm under the surface diving for starfish and sea urchin, I could care less how cold it is outside."

"What's the temperature of the water?" I asked.

"Thirty-six degrees. My dry suit keeps the cold at bay—well, it modifies it. I went through four tanks today and I could feel my core temperature slowly dropping. It can be exhausting this time of year."

While I examined the children for their physicals, Dave kept up a running commentary on what he viewed as the dangers of gentrification on Peaks versus "old" Peaks Island. His voice dropped to a whisper. "If you look carefully at the zoning for our neighborhood, I think some-one could make a stink about the formaldehyde we use to preserve our specimens. We have great neighbors, but. . ." He cracked open a book he was reading, *The Peninsula* by Louise Dickinson Rich, and pointed a finger to a paragraph: *In Winter Harbor. . . no one there ever sets out (lob-ster) traps. They were all too busy washing the windows, clipping the hedges, and raking the driveways of the wealthy. I don't blame them for choosing this easier means of making a better living, but I cannot help feeling they have sold their birthright. . . They have thrown away their independence.*

Peaks was far from a traditional fishing island, the morning ferry to Portland was full of commuters, but there were parallels between *The Peninsula* and recent changes on Peaks. "At some point, we might move up the coast," Dave continued. "Isle au Haut is one possibility. The island has only sixty or so year-round residents and they've developed a Homestead Program to attract young families. It's a great deal; they provide a community-built home on a rent to buy program. Penobscot bay would be ideal for our business. If we qualify, we just might go."

A half-hour later, I watched silently as Dave bundled the children up and disappeared into a white-out. The double-hung windows on the north side of the cottage rattled as a blast of polar wind shook the building. I looked at my watch; there would be a rash of cancellations today. That was okay, I had plenty of paperwork to catch up on. Maybe I'd have enough free time to read a medical journal article.

So, I was genuinely surprised when the front door creaked open and there was Johnny Dinsmore tapping his way in with a gnarled cane. Somehow, the diminutive Irishman had survived his rib fractures, flail chest, and ten days on a ventilator last fall. By the time his chest tube was pulled, his chief complaint was constipation from the narcotics. Less than three weeks after he'd been pinned under his van and mostly dead, he was discharged on Tylenol. He's been left with a pug nose, a permanently deviated right eye (from an orbital fracture), and a foot drop secondary to trauma to the peroneal nerve. I hoped he was not driving his van.

Collapsing into a chair, Johnny wrestled a boot off and propped a swollen foot up on the cushion. Oh no, not another bout of the gout. Before he could settle in, Anne helped him to his feet and suggested he follow her into the exam room. Between his deviated eye, the foot drop, and the inflammation lurking beneath his pants, Johnny lurched after Anne like a leprechaun zombie.

I stuck a bookmark in the journal article and placed it in my backpack. Inside the room, Johnny pulled up his pants leg. The knees and ankles were so warm and swollen, they reminded me of taut water balloons ready to burst. His index finger dripped chalky gouty uric acid through a filthy band-aid. The great toe looked like the least of his problems.

Johnny groaned, his eyes half-closed. "My gout's been quiet for months. I had to know if it was the black cherry treatment or the pills you give me." I was thinking, *No, you didn't have to know.* "So, when I ran out of the prescription pills, I figured it was the right time to stop taking them." *No, it's never the right time.* "For a few days, I took a swig of black cherry juice every morning and thought I was on the right track." *No you weren't on the right track.*

"The store changed brands of black cherry juice last month," Johnny continued. "I noticed a few days ago, it had a bitter taste. Do you think that's the problem?" He looked up from rubbing his knee with a look of genuine curiosity.

Ignoring the question, I made up my mind, "Johnny, how do you feel about me numbing up the skin, drawing the gout fluid out of both knees and ankles, and injecting cortisone?"

"Me? What do I know? You're the doctor."

Yes. I'm the doctor, I thought, *but, apparently, so is my schizophrenic patient Ruth.* Okay, that was not necessarily accurate. Ruth suggested the black cherry juice, but I went along with it in the vain hope that it would improve Johnny's compliance with prescription medications.

Four separate aspirations and injections later, I ducked my head out the door and was surprised to see Lois Herndon following Anne into the adjacent exam room. What could bring Lois out, unscheduled, on a day like this? She turned slightly before the door shut and in silhouette her face was pale and drawn, like she'd heard bad news, like maybe she *was* the bad news. In all the time I'd known her, through the ups and downs of vasculitis, this was the first time I'd sensed that her genteel wit had deserted her.

Johnny stood on bowed legs and flexed his knees up and down. "Say . . . that's better already. My gout medicines came down yesterday on the afternoon ferry and I filled the pillbox with allopurinol. I was waiting for you to give me the okay."

I looked at him skeptically. "You'll go back on the daily allopurinol?"

"Of course. Now that I know it was doing the trick."

"Okay," I wrote out my instructions. "First, don't start on full-strength allopurinol. Cut the pills in half for the first week before going back to one pill each day. And add one of the colchicine to the daily allopurinol until I see you back in two weeks. It's a recipe, like. . . making soup. To make it right, you need the proper mix of the correct ingredients."

Johnny slowly read my instructions back to me and placed them in his wallet before shuffling out to the front window. Anne pulled me aside and whispered, "Do you think a Community Health nurse could help Johnny stay on track with his medications? They'll need an order."

I pulled out my prescription pad and quickly scribbled out the prescription. "Of course. That's perfect. Thanks so much."

I turned my attention to Lois. She barely looked up as I sat down on a stool inside her exam room. "What can I do for you today, Lois?"

In reply, she lifted the side of her blouse to reveal a football-sized bruise extending over her lateral chest wall toward the back. I auscultated her lungs and heart. Thankfully, they were okay. Placing a hand gently over the bruise, I asked her to take a breath. She winced as I felt a grating sensation beneath my hand. She'd broken several ribs.

"Can you tell me what happened?" I asked.

"Do you promise to keep it a secret?"

"Yes."

"I tripped and fell into the lobster trap coffee table in my living room last night. The glass shattered, but miraculously, I don't seem to have a scratch on me."

"Well, that's fortunate."

"I wish that were so." There was a long pause before she went on. "Like I said, I fell into the lobster trap. Backwards. Butt first." Lois lifted her head and winced. "I was trapped by the trap." I tried unsuccessfully to stifle a laugh. A moment later, Lois giggled and groaned, holding the side of her chest, as tears ran down her cheeks. "I must have looked like an upside-down Galapagos turtle struggling to right itself. The best I could do was roll onto my side, my butt still inside the trap. I think that's when I heard a rib crack. Somehow, I slid out of the trap and crawled into my bed."

"You what? You didn't get checked out in town?" I asked.

"Think about it. In two minutes, you've diagnosed me with fractured ribs. Last night, if I called 911, the police would arrive at my house and pack me into the ambulance and rattle down the potholes of Welch Street and roll me over the gangplank onto the fireboat. I get seasick on the trip to town, transfer to *another* ambulance, and arrive in the emergency room, where they'd take an x-ray and tell this old broad, 'You have a fractured rib.'"

I started to laugh again but caught myself. "I'm certainly glad to see you Lois. You do know, there's not much I can do except treat your pain."

"As if that's not enough to win the Nobel Prize!" Lois answered, shifting uncomfortably in her chair. "I didn't sleep a wink last night."

"Okay. I'm going to start you on hydrocodone; it should take the edge off." I reached up over the sink and unlocked the medicine cabinet and counted out fifteen pills and placed them in a plastic vial. Then I half-filled a paper cup and handed her several to take before the ride home. "Sometimes narcotics can affect your balance," I cautioned her, "particularly at night. Is there someone who can stay with you the next few nights, help you up to the bathroom, make sure you don't fall? The last thing we want is for you to trip and fracture a hip."

"I think so. I can talk to my neighbor Julie; she's always been very helpful."

"Great. Here you're finally off prednisone for your giant cell arteritis, and . . . I'm really sorry," I said, shaking my head. "You've had a tough year. How'd you get to the health center? Please don't say you walked."

"Island taxi."

"If you wait a few minutes, I'll take you home in the truck. The snow is piling up; we're closing shortly."

"Are you going to the meeting tonight at the community room?" Lois asked. "There's a vote on whether we'll have a hunt this winter to thin the deer herd."

"Another meeting?" I looked up from writing my note. "Community meetings are worse than useless."

"I think there's a good chance this time will be different. Now that several families have set up feeding stations to help the poor starving deer, most islanders have had enough. Did you see the comment Jenny Yasi wrote in this week's island newsletter?" Lois pulled out the paper from her purse and found the quote. 'I can tell you if there were rats instead of deer swarming all over this island, there'd be no discussion over a hunt.' I'm telling you, this time the Bambi crowd might not carry the day."

While Lois sat in the waiting room, I helped Anne close up the clinic. Then I gathered my supplies and led Lois down the outside ramp to the truck and climbed inside and turned on the heater. After starting the truck, I pulled out my pocket calendar and wrote, *Specimens to lab. Deer meeting?* There was a knock. Through the open window, Lois peered back at me like I was the village idiot. She didn't need to say a word; anyone with a lick of sense would know that an elderly woman with fractured ribs can't pull herself up into a truck. I could feel my Nobel Prize slipping away.

"I'm sorry. I'm really sorry," I stammered. "I don't know what I was thinking. Can I . . . walk you home?" In response, Lois lightly touched my elbow and half closed her eyes and pointed me in the direction of her cottage. We shuffled along the shoulder of the deserted road as the snow drifted down. A raven croaked overhead. A loose dog showed no interest in us. A boy dragging a sled ran by, oblivious to everything except the promise of the hill at the end of Elizabeth Street.

We navigated the three stairs to her front door and, once inside, I was able to help Lois into her recliner. Her neighbor Julie arrived unannounced and heated up a pot of steaming tea. Robert and Jerry from across the street brought over pumpkin soup. On his way out, Robert cleaned up the broken lobster trap from the living room, disposed of the glass, and kept the rest for firewood. On the way out he said, "Lois, you're a tough old broad."

"Thank you," Lois replied. "I *am* a tough old broad."

19

Six weeks later, on a breezy April Sunday morning, I picked up Bobby Emerson in my truck and drove onto our beach on an outgoing tide. Patches of snow held on in the deeper shade of the beach grass. The down-the-bay ferry glided by across the channel, hugging the deeper water off Little Diamond Island.

Bobby grabbed his Skilsaw and ran a long extension cord to an outlet beside my back door. In the bed of my truck was a load of 16-foot marine lumber, three rectangular vinyl plastic floats, four marine cast-iron cleats, and enough angle iron, stainless-steel screws, washers, and nuts to fasten my float together. Arranging our materials on the upper beach, Bobby estimated we had six hours before the tide rose and flooded our workspace.

Bobby rolled up his sleeves and trimmed the boards to size on the edge of the truck's tailgate, his Skilsaw ripping through the marine lumber like butter. I methodically drilled and set the angle iron, washers, and nuts. Pete, my next-door neighbor, wandered down to the beach and helped us flip the frame so that we could attach the plastic floats to the underbelly. Then, another neighbor out walking his dog asked if we needed help. We did. The four of us grunted and heaved the float right-side up. Only then did it cross my mind that three years ago, I'd transferred Bobby off the island by fireboat in complete heart block. Last summer, at age 73, he'd fished five hundred traps, his only concession, a sternman to help with hauling and baiting. Bobby looked over his work. "Go grab your boat. By the time we move the truck off the beach, the tide will be high enough to drag your float into the water."

On board SAKAMO, I was only too aware of a topic I'd purposefully avoided with Bobby, the recent deer hunt. After a tumultuous meeting at the library, the city had agreed to hire a sharpshooter to thin the herd. There were dissenters. My friend Gary Gustafson, who opposed the sharpshooter plan, was quoted by the newspaper, saying, "The City Council voted for killing, so now we have killing." On some issues, there simply can be no agreement.

A few days before the scheduled hunt, Bobby and two other men were arrested for poaching. Following a tip, game wardens followed a trail of blood into the basement of Bobby's house and discovered four dead does. They confiscated the deer for evidence and Bobby eventually paid a substantial fine. I knew exactly what Bobby was thinking: *They're going to shoot the deer anyway. Why should I lose out on a freezer full of venison?*

Following the arrests, after baiting a remote area in the island's interior, the state sharpshooter shot 172 deer over five nights. That's a lot of deer. Peaks Island is slightly more than a mile across and four miles around. That worked out to about seventy deer per square mile. And there were still deer remaining on the island; I surprised a buck on my run yesterday on the trail circling the beaver pond.

When he saw me approaching the beach in *SAKAMO*, Bobby waded into the water and threw me a line. I tied off the line to a stern clean and pulled the float off the beach. An hour later, after attaching the hardware connecting my float to his, we sat on the edge of the Army wharf nursing a beer. I couldn't stop thanking the man. I handed him an open bag of chips and asked, "I heard the sharpshooter was busy last month. Did he really shoot 172 deer?"

Bobby stared out over the water, "Seems a little low, maybe closer to 180 were harvested." Bobby pointed toward House Island a quarter mile offshore. "Look, midway between the old house and the fort. Up from the beach, a buck and two does. There's probably a fawn or two in the underbrush. They'll be over here before you know it."

My curiosity got the better of me. I wanted to know more about Bobby's arrest. "When the game warden found four deer in your basement, I don't understand why they bothered to charge you. I mean, in another week, the same deer would have been killed by the sharpshooter. Did they let you keep the meat after you paid the fine?"

"Nope, but that's no matter. They found four deer in my basement. That's illegal." Bobby stopped for a moment and kicked a dead crab off the pier. "Ever tasted fresh venison?"

I shook my head. "No."

"Nothing like it. It's a weakness of mine." Bobby stood and stretched. "Like I said, 172 deer shot seems a little low, maybe closer to 180 were harvested."

Rick Crowley parked his truck one-handed at the base of the wharf and strolled down to where we were standing. Despite the cool breeze, Rick wore a T-shirt and light jeans with unlaced boots. A bulky cast extended from his mid-upper left arm past his flexed elbow and included the wrist and all but the last several inches of his fingers. "Check this out, Dr. Radis. I've got some movement back already." I leaned in for a closer look. Rick grimaced as he attempted to flex the fingers. Only the index finger had a hint of movement. I forced a smile of encouragement.

"Dr. Barr is going to check me out next week," Rick said, accepting a beer. "If he's satisfied the tendon attachments are holding, he'll saw off the cast. Then I'm good to go." While we chatted, Bobby walked down to the beach and dragged Rick's dinghy from where it was stored above the high tide and tied it to the far end of my float. Rick's blue eyes darted toward where his scallop boat was moored. "Say, how about you motor me out to *E Cosi*? When the Coast Guard transferred me to Portland couple of months ago, I didn't get a chance to lock the hatch leading to the engine compartment. I need to check and see if there's water in the hold."

I hesitated. It seemed risky. Then I reluctantly agreed. Without another word, Rick opened the gate and started down the ladder to my float one-handed. "Hey, wait a minute Rick! Careful!" I scrambled down after him.

"This will take only a minute. I've got this."

But I was too late. Rick was already on my float. Steadying himself, he grasped the bar extending off the pilot house of *SAKAMO* and jumped aboard. By the time I boarded and started the engine, I was fuming. I pointed to a life jacket. "We're not going anywhere until you put your life jacket on. You've already torn up—"

"Fine, you're the captain." Rick shrugged his shoulders and wiggled into a life jacket and somehow secured the fasteners. A few minutes later, as I nudged up against *E Cosi*, Rick abruptly stood on the rail, and over my objections, pulled himself onto his boat one-handed, lifted up the hatch, and disappeared into the hold. Moments later, he was back on deck, smiling widely. "The engine's fine. No water in the hold. Now I can get some sleep." A few minutes later, back on my float, he retraced his one-handed route up the ladder, and drove off.

That night, as Sandi and I lay in bed, I told her I understood why she enjoyed plumbing and electrical work so much. "You begin with a plan and a bucket of replacement parts and when you're done, you've created something tangible. Just like my project with Bobby today."

Sandi patted my arm. "Are you trying to tell me something? Don't tell me you're thinking of giving up medicine? Before flipping the light off, she scrutinized me more closely, then nestled in closer and whispered. "We don't need two bad backs." In a few minutes she was asleep. I picked up my pocket calendar and pen from the bureau, and in the glow of the night-light in the bathroom wrote: *New admission. Bring skin biopsy kit to hospital.* Even with the satisfaction of building the float, my mind was pivoting. As I drifted off, I realized each patient is a project. Some were repaired as good as new. Others, despite my best efforts, fell apart before the next visit. There was no predicting how long the repairs would last.

Early the following morning, as a light mist crept in from the open ocean, I bicycled down front, and purchased a cup of coffee at Lisa's on my way to the Army Pier. After stowing my backpack and green satchel, I turned the key and released the lines. Compared to rowing out to my mooring, it was almost too easy.

My first stop at the hospital was to evaluate a 13-year-old girl with a purpuric, blotchy rash on her lower extremities, anemia, and symmetric small joint polyarthritis. Late last night I'd agreed to accept the admission through the ER, thinking the illness represented a severe viral syndrome. This morning, the night intern refreshed me with the details of the case. He had started an IV, given her meds for pain, and drawn blood for additional studies. I was disturbed that the young woman's white blood count and platelets were low and her creatinine, a measure of kidney function, was slightly elevated. I was particularly concerned about the elevated creatinine. Dehydration can do that, I thought to myself, but so can an inflammatory process in the kidney. "Did you order a urinalysis, sed rate, CRP, and a fresh CBC and creatinine for this morning?" I asked.

"Yes, they're pending." He tucked in his scrubs with one hand as he finished the last of his admission note. As I entered the room with the intern, the girl's parents roused themselves from their chairs where they'd briefly dozed off. We shook hands. I reviewed the history the intern had shared with me and asked a number of follow-up questions while their daughter slept.

A rash extended from both cheeks across the bridge of her nose. Her respiratory rate was elevated. Her lips were dried and cracked. I lightly nudged her hand and her eyes opened. "Hello Amanda, I'm Doctor Radis, mind if I sit down?" She locked eyes with her mother and nodded warily. I took a seat on the edge of the bed and asked to see her hands. The wrists and nearly all of the knuckles of both hands were swollen. She winced when I gently palpated the individual joints. I clicked on my pen light and asked Amanda to open her mouth. On the right lateral aspect of the tongue was a large ulcer. Below the knees, a rash, varying in size between a pin head and a dime was present. Several of the lesions were ulcerated and painful to the touch.

The inflamed joints, rash, and tongue ulcer all pointed toward systemic lupus erythematosus. Without a word, the intern handed me the results of the repeat morning lab. The numbers were not reassuring. The creatinine was trending upwards, and the urinalysis, with large amounts of protein and blood, pointed toward damage to the kidneys. Amanda's blood counts were in the dumpster; all three cell lines--white blood cells, red blood cells, and platelets—were trending lower. I asked the intern to call the lab and have them run a haptoglobin, ANA, double-stranded DNA, and C3 and C4 from the blood draw earlier this morning.

Across town, the Tuesday morning conference was already underway. Paulding Phelps, the chief of rheumatology, gave me a thumbs up when he noticed me take a seat in the back. When I was done presenting 13-year-old Amanda's case Dr. Phelps said, "Sick girl. Do you have any thoughts?"

"I think she has lupus, probably with a small vessel vasculitis, glo-merulonephritis, and hemolytic anemia." I looked around the confer-ence room; there was general agreement.

"What have you done so far?" Dr. Phelps asked.

"She had her first dose of Solu-medrol about an hour ago. I gave her a conservative dose, thinking that if she needs a kidney biopsy, a high dose might affect the results of the biopsy. I have an uneasy feel-ing about her, like the bottom's going to fall out. Even her chest x-ray, which was read as normal, looks troubling. I placed the morning's x-ray on the viewing box. "By my eye, there's a subtle infiltrate in both lower lung fields."

"Thank you, Dr. Radis." Dr. Phelps pointed out the infiltrates to the medical residents and added, "Sometimes lupus unfolds over months, or even years. Other times, the disease takes off like a rocket, and it's a medical emergency. I agree with Dr. Radis, this young woman is in trouble. Even without the benefit of further immuno-logic labs, she undoubtedly has lupus and needs aggressive medical management."

"Which brings me to my next concern," I said. "I'm not a pediatri-cian and I'm certainly not a pediatric rheumatologist; would one of you accept her as a transfer later today?"

Dr. Larry Anderson spoke up first. "Sure. I'm on call this week for the group and I can make the arrangements to accept the transfer later afternoon. In the meantime, Chuck, why don't you order a thousand milligrams of IV Solu-medrol for your patient? I think that's important to get on board. I'll call nephrology to see if they can schedule her for a kidney biopsy tomorrow morning; a day or two of high-dose steroids won't affect the histology.

At the end of the conference, I was on my way out the door when Dr. Phelps pulled me aside. "Good summary." He stopped for a moment, choosing his words carefully. "So . . . how's the practice on Peaks Island and in town? If you haven't noticed, you're becoming the de facto rheumatologist for the osteopathic community."

"It's good. Hectic, but good."

"I know you did most of your electives in rheumatology during your residency, so you have an excellent knowledge base. You've been coming to our conference for the better part of five years. Have you ever considered doing a rheumatology fellowship?"

"Well, yes and no. I knew that when I finished my internal medicine training, that wasn't an option. I went through osteopathic medical school on a National Health Service Corp. scholarship and needed to practice in a health manpower shortage area. That's why I chose the Casco Bay islands. Best decision I ever made. But I've always had an interest in immunology and autoimmune disease. I remember that the first introductory course I took at Bates College in 1973 was taught by Dr. Andy Balber. At the time, I remember Dr. Balber clicking on a blank slide on the projector and commenting, 'This is what we know about T cell surface receptors. Almost nothing.' It was if he were challenging the class to get cracking and fill in the blanks. Years later, I heard that a number of us gravitated to medicine or basic science immunology."

"Well, maybe now is the time you circled back," Dr. Phelps said. "I think you'd be a good candidate for a fellowship. You're out of synch for interviews; the new fellows have been picked to start their programs later this summer. On the other hand, sometimes the programs, even excellent programs, don't always fill their slots."

"Aren't I a little old for a fellowship?"

"Not really. How old are you?"

"Thirty-eight."

"Let me make a few calls, and I'll get back to you."

"Sure. I'd appreciate that." Outside in my truck, I pulled out my pocket calendar and wrote: *Meet with family. Order Solu-medrol. Transfer patient.*

2 0

D an Durgin, the volunteer coordinator for Pond Grove cemetery, waved down my truck as he emerged from Feeney's Market nibbling on a Mallomar cookie. "Want to meet your neighbors? I can meet you at the front gate in twenty minutes."

Hurrying home, I found Sandi upstairs at her sewing machine repairing a zipper on Molly's raincoat. "This could be really weird," she said. Do we have to do this today?"

"More than a year after we first asked about a burial plot? Yes, I think we need to do this today."

Back in the truck, we drove up Central Avenue until the road devolved from macadam to packed dirt. I pulled up at the wrought iron cemetery gate. Considering that we're both in our late thirties, our decision to look into burial plots on the island might have seemed premature, but it was triggered by Sandi's practicality; there was only one "active" cemetery on the island, and it was running out of room.

When our friend Jean visited Peaks from Boston, she enjoyed relaxing at Brackett Memorial Cemetery on the south side of the island. It's a spectacular setting looking out on cresting waves rolling in from the open ocean, clanging buoys, and a cliff where nesting guillemots reside. When she heard we were looking into plots in Pond Grove cemetery in the center of Peaks, she said to Sandi, "I'm disappointed. I was looking forward to visiting your graves at Bracket cemetery. Now what am I going to do?"

"What makes you so sure we'll die before you do?" Sandi asked.

Of course, Brackett, was "closed" so Jean's preference was moot. The grounds at Pond Grove have an orderly, small town feel to them. It was a popular spot for Kate and Molly's friends' after-dinner games of kick the can and hide and seek. The Memorial Day parade in which Sandi played her clarinet ended at Pond Grove.

183

The connection was even stronger for me; a number of my favorite patients were buried in Pond Grove. I often cut through Pond Grove near the end of a long run, and the headstones triggered memories that might have otherwise faded. As another small-town physician, Kathryn Rinsenbrenck, once wrote, "it is a peculiar privilege of a rural doctor to walk among one's dead."

We pulled up at the gate and Dan motioned us inside. Flat grassy mounds identified each grave site where soil was heaped up from the granite bedrock. Stands of pointed fir and red spruce edged the rectangular open space. Here and there, the backyards of pastel-colored cottages could be seen through the dense woods. Coming to a stop, Dan gestured toward a grassy plot where two moss-covered paths converged. "Here it is. Your plot."

Heads bowed, Sandi and I stared intently at our site, a gentle mound for two, unsure what to say next. "It's a nice spot," Sandi offered.

"You're on the corner, prime real estate," Dan replied. "Lorie Gamble, she's already planted next to Sandi. Lorie always liked her cocktails at five so it's possible you'll be in on that."

"And next to me?" I asked.

"Samuel Fear. Folks say he always had a crush on Lorie. I didn't know Samuel well. Nobody really did. Bachelor lobsterman. Dr. Radis, you may have doctored him at the health center for some kind of skin disease; his hands were always festered up. Got so that most folks didn't want to shake his hand."

Dan quietly reviewed the price of admission to Pond Grove cemetery and said we could drop off a check at his house anytime. That was it; there was nothing more to say. He slowly made his way back to his truck while Sandi and I wandered among the tombstones. Dan's family plot was almost immediately behind ours. Adjacent to theirs, Henry Meyers' headstone proclaimed: *He worked for peace.* Hilda Milton, a home-bound woman I doctored unsuccessfully for years with a chronic lower leg ulcer, was finally out of her house. Lockhart Blaney, a kind, melancholic patient with a memorable name, rested across the lane.

The haunting call of a piliated woodpecker echoed over the neatly mowed grounds. We left Pond Grove on a narrow dirt path lined with wild geranium. At the cemetery's edge a framed, water-stained photo of a young woman leaned against the trunk of a sugar maple. There was a spent candle next to the photo and a bouquet of oxbow daisies on the dry leaves. A red crayon note was tucked inside a plastic bag with the photo. *Miss you forever. Love, Jen.*

"Drug overdose," Sandi said simply.

"I know," I said, pushing my glasses up on my forehead and rubbing my eyes. "I remember." We walked quietly on, circling the cemetery back to the truck.

The next morning, I stopped to admire our front field. A bushy stand of orange-flowered jewelweed lined the walkway. On slightly higher ground, Canadian goldenrod and bull thistle were in full bloom. At least once a week, I pulled bindweed out by the roots where it threatened to overrun the lupines I'd planted several years ago. It was probably a losing battle; the soil and sun exposure weren't a perfect match for the lupine. Perhaps this summer I'd work a few seeds into the ground on the edge of the field nearer the road. As I veered into Snake Alley across from the school, I realized that I hadn't seen a deer in three months. Jack in-the-pulpit, turtlehead, and sensitive fern—plants I haven't seen in years—were reclaiming the shadowy understory.

Recharged, I stopped at the outside door to the health center and readied myself for morning clinic. I walked across the waiting room; I was ten minutes early, but the room was nearly full. Anne led Sister Mia into an exam room, bypassing the scale. Marcia Quinby was there, and so was a young woman I was treating for chronic anxiety. Nicholas Slater, a long-time summer resident, appeared sweaty and short of breath where he stood leaning on the back of a chair.

From my desk, I leaned back to observe Mr. Slater. After his successful intestinal bypass surgery several years ago, he'd dropped more than 100 pounds. Last summer, he hadn't needed the services of the health center, but I saw him several times moving easily along without a cane. Today, I estimate his weight at north of 300 pounds, perhaps exceeding his pre-intestinal bypass weight. *What went wrong?*

On my way in the door to see Sister Mia, I told Anne, "Room Mr. Slater next. If his vitals are out of line, knock on my door. I have a bad feeling about him."

"You don't want me to call the police? Mike and Big John are on today and I can call the fireboat."

"No, not yet. That would create a scene, and Mr. Slater may refuse to go to town. Let me check him out first. Oh, and do a finger prick on him for a blood sugar while I'm in with Sister Mia."

Sister Mia grasped my hand in hers as I entered the exam room. "It seems that the Lord has one last gift in store for me. Saint Josephs by the Sea is closing, and the diocese is moving me and the remaining sisters to a new retirement convent in Massachusetts. Around the corner is an orphanage where I will, God willing, teach in the grade school. Forty years ago, I taught in an orphanage in Brazil. I was quite content there." For a moment, Sister Mia's complex medical problems melted away. She was once again a vibrant young nun; energetic, whip-smart, and critically necessary.

"You're moving away?" I slumped backward in my chair. Sister Mia reached over and squeezed my hand. I remembered how several years ago, her steady presence and spiritual advice had helped an anorexic teenager survive through the darkest times. Even when he'd regressed into cutting himself, her faith in his recovery never wavered. There's no question she played a critical role in his recovery.

"When are you and the sisters leaving?" I asked.

"Later this week. All of the arrangements have been quietly made. Father Stevens has told us that a small order of monks is moving to Peaks Island to live in our quarters."

"Retired monks?"

"Yes, retired monks. I'm told they make beer."

"Retired monks making beer?"

"Dr. Radis," Sister Mia looked at me sharply. Just because the prospect of teaching orphans softened the blow of moving off Peaks Island, didn't mean she had lost her prickly side. "I will say this once more. They are retired, but they are not drunkards. They will be of assistance to the community. And yes, they make their own beer." Discussion closed. I could almost feel her blood pressure rising. Despite her openness to moving to Massachusetts, I sensed that if it were up to her, she would have preferred to live out her years on Peaks Island. She abruptly changed the subject. "I notice you've been running again."

"Yes, I had a wake-up call."

She smiled knowingly. There was no doubt in my mind that she knew the details of my cardiac catheterization. "I'm pleased that you are making the time to run. When I was young, I loved the feel of the earth moving beneath my feet. Then I was ordered to stop and walk. In my last years, I'll make sure the children under my care feel the joy of movement." Abruptly, Sister Mia stood, embraced me in a long bear hug, and limped to the checkout window to say goodbye to Anne.

Pulling back the shade, I watched the elderly nun shuffle across the parking lot and pull herself into the passenger seat. Sister Marie Henry, her head barely level with the steering wheel, waved in my direction. Abruptly, the van exploded into reverse, knocking down the neighbor's rail fence. I opened my pocket calendar and wrote: *Sister Mia needs new doctor in Massachusetts.* I watched the dust settle and wrote: *Warn retirement home that Sister Marie-Henry lacks driver's license.*

The chair across the hall was considerably wider than any in the waiting room, wide enough to accommodate Mr. Slater. On this unusually warm July morning, he wore a velour chocolate-colored hat, corduroy pants, sockless loafers, and a black, expansive T-shirt inscribed with: *CHESS:* Where the Elite Meet.

"How can I help you today, Mr. Slater?"

"I seem to be inordinately . . . short of breath." The simple words required a quick, almost imperceptible second breath between "inordinately" and "short:" four-word dyspnea, not a good sign. I auscultated Mr. Slater's heart and lungs. His forehead was moist and wet crackles were present in both lower lung fields. His heart was racing at one-hundred-fifteen beats per minute. Elephantine pitting edema reaching up to his mid-calves. *Congestive heart failure. Call the fireboat.*

Through the open door I motioned for Anne to set in motion the transfer before grabbing the spare oxygen tank and setting the flow at two liters per minute, then quietly inserted an IV into his forearm and injected a dose of furosemide, a diuretic. Throughout this, Mr. Slater seemed oddly disconnected to the pace of events, sucking on a mint and staring listlessly at the far wall.

The police arrived. Officers Mike Barter and Big John assessed the situation through the lens of: *How are we going to deliver this man to the fireboat?* And it was true, while Mr. Slater seemed to have walked under his own power into the health center after taking the island taxi, the effort seemed to tip him over into a helpless, exhausted state. His fingertips were an ominous dusky blue. I increased the oxygen to three liters per minute.

Officer Mike retrieved the stretcher from the ambulance and rolled it in through the back entrance. There was no room for the stretcher in the exam room. Anne handed me the results of Mr. Slater's blood sugar: 335 mg/dl. At this, Mr. Slater's head bobbed up and he said, "Good god, that number matches my weight!"

Big John stepped behind Mr. Slater and announced he was going to help him walk to the stretcher. It was only about ten feet. Big John reached under Mr. Slater's armpits and lifted him to a standing position and dance-walked the big man to the stretcher. For all of the assistance Mr. Slater provided, he may as well have been a sack of potatoes. Mike and I each grabbed a leg and swung them on to the stretcher. Oxygen running. Nasal cannula in place. In another minute, Mr. Slater was on his way.

I summarized the visit in Mr. Slater's chart. Before addressing my next patient, I unwrapped a Snickers bar and downed the remainder of my second cup of coffee. I realized I didn't know if Mr. Slater would choose to be hospitalized at the osteopathic hospital under my care or at Maine Medical Center. If the latter, I'd call cardiologist Charlie Hoag to give him a heads up. Then I picked up the chart of Marcia Quinby and knocked lightly on the door before entering.

"Good morning, Marcia. A little excitement here today."

"I can see that," Marcia smiled back. "I won't keep you long. The carpal tunnel syndrome and tendonitis in my wrist is gone. I'm sleeping better and off the anti-inflammatory; the wrist splint really helps. Normally, I would have rescheduled, but I wanted you to know before you heard it through the community grapevine; David and I are moving up the coast to Isle au Haut early next month."

"Without the children?" I deadpanned, trying to hide my disappointment.

"Very funny. Of course, with the children. It was a big decision, but between the worries we have about our neighbors someday objecting to our use of formalin preservative in the barn and the homestead program Isle au Haut is offering, we didn't think we should pass it up. David is optimistic that our dive business will thrive in Penobscot Bay; he'll have an easier time collecting sufficient starfish and sea urchin specimens for Carolina Biologic Supply.

"From what I understand, your three children will double the number of students in the Isle au Haut school."

"We're hoping we won't be the only new family on the island. But to be truthful, we don't fear isolation. Our family has always been self-contained. We'll do just fine. We're renting out our house on Peaks, so if it's a bad match, we can always move back."

While Marcia talked, I flexed and tapped the right wrist and examined it for swelling or tenderness. It was back to normal. We sat quietly for a moment. The Quinbys' family business epitomized the wild-west era of Peaks Island. I could see that time coming to an end. On the new Peaks Island, work boats pulled up above the high-tide mark for repairs might not be welcome. Junk cars, unable to pass inspection on the mainland, could be prohibited. Life wouldn't be necessarily better or worse, just different. Still, I'd miss the grittiness of families like the Quinbys.

"I heard the nuns are leaving," Marcia interrupted my daydreaming.

"Several monks are moving into their house," I nodded. "One of them is blind; he has a guide dog."

"Is it true they make their own beer?" Marcia asked.

"Good question," I replied. "If you run into Sister Mia, you might ask her about the beer."

That evening, I laid out a dress shirt and tartan green tie and shined my work shoes for the first time in, well, ever. I was scheduled tomorrow for a rheumatology fellowship interview at Presbyterian Medical Center in Pittsburgh. If all went well, I'd take *SAKAMO* in for an early flight from Portland and return to the island by bedtime. I pulled out my pocket calendar and wrote: *200 Lothrop St, conference room 276, Tom Medsger, Chief of Rheumatology.*

Before bed, Sandi asked me to tuck the plane ticket to Pittsburgh in the side pocket of my green satchel. "You remember where we keep the extra key for the car in town?"

"In the magnetized case in the wheel well."

"Good. Can you call me when you land in Pittsburgh?"

"I will." I switched on a nightlight and scribbled the reminder in my pocket calendar.

A few minutes later, Sandi turned on her nightlight. "I understand why you're interviewing, but that doesn't mean we should go if you're accepted. Moving is traumatic. It's traumatic for me and it's traumatic for Kate and Molly. You've noticed the dozen or so boxes I have stored in the attic? After we moved into this house five years ago, I thought this might be our last move. Now you're telling me I might need those boxes again."

"You've kept those boxes all these years?" I asked.

"Every time I think of throwing them away, I hold off. It seems like bad luck. Peaks is a good place to raise our children. We have friends we can rely on. We're finally settled in, and except for the nuisance of frozen pipes, I like our house. We've moved more than enough for one lifetime. Here's a question. How many times did we move between your second year of medical school and graduation?"

I was close to dozing off. "I don't know, maybe four or five times?"

"Nine." There was a long silence before Sandi said, "Sure, some of those were one-month clinical rotations in Cleveland or Chicago or southern Missouri, but we were constantly on the go. How many times did we move on Peaks before Kate was three years old?"

I was fully alert now. "I remember we rented the first nine months, then we bought this house. Twice?" Before the words were out of my mouth, I knew that I should have at least doubled that number.

"Five times. We rented the first nine months, then we bought this house, and camped here for a summer. The property was so overgrown with alders and bittersweet you could barely see the house from the road. There was no insulation in the walls and the knob and tube wiring beneath the horse-hair plaster was a fire hazard. Lois Herndon was kind enough to let us live in her house while she was away in Greece. That was our third move. When Lois returned, renovations were months behind schedule, so we moved into the Dahls' house down by Tre-fethen. Early the next spring, we moved back in here. That's five moves. Now you're telling me we might move again? To a city? To Pittsburgh?"

The word Pittsburgh drifted overhead like an accusation. I was not contemplating a move up the coast to Isle au Haut with a year-round population of sixty, I was interviewing for a fellowship in rheumatology and clinical immunology in a city of 1.7 million. Of course, if we went, the great unknown was whether our family would fare better or worse in Pittsburgh. I'd read that the city is relatively safe, but there was no way Kate would bicycle or free-range outdoors in Pittsburgh like she did on Peaks. Could Molly roller skate in front of the house? Five children were in Kate's first-grade class this year. How would she fare in a crowded inner-city public school? If Sandi worked, would she gravitate back to counseling or toward plumbing and electrician work?

I brushed a swatch of Sandi's hair over her ear. "Let's at least see where this interview leads. Even though I keep making adjustments in my schedule, and there's no doubt *SAKAMO* has helped smooth out my commute, I'm still working seventy-plus hours a week."

Sandi sat up and adjusted the pillow behind her back. She was in her problem-solving mode. "Can you explain to me again why you can't limit your practice to Peaks Island? Why can't we make that work?" Sandi payed the bills in our family and tracked our savings. We were in the black, but not exactly rolling in cash.

"Yes, we're doing okay, but most of that is from the income from my in-town and hospital practice. On Peaks, this is the first year after subtracting the cost of medical and office supplies and the rent for the clinic building, that I've cleared more than what I pay Anne. There simply aren't enough people on the Peaks to support a full-time practice."

"And there's this; when I think about my most challenging patients, I keep circling back to the rare immune-system diseases they developed, seemingly out of the blue. When I have a spare moment to read, it's rheumatology journals I read. I'd like to take care of those people instead of turning them over to the rheumatologists. If all goes well, we could come back after two years in Pittsburgh and I could join the group.

Sandi raised an eyebrow. "And live here?"

"Somebody's got to keep the pipes from freezing."

The next morning, the bay was a flat tropical blue. The summit of Mount Washington was visible above the northwest horizon seventy miles distant. A coating of dew clung to the cattails drooping across our boardwalk as I pushed my bike up to the road. Outside her coffee shop, Lisa propped the door open for the early-morning ferry commuters. I watched Rick Crowley and a bearded young man in a yellow-hooded sweatshirt wrestle Rick's dinghy off my float and into the water. Recognizing me, Rick shouted, "I have the contracts to maintain the moorings off your beach and another dozen off Trefethan. For now, that'll be enough to keep Nancy and me out of the poor house!" I was flat out amazed. Who would guess after his gruesome accident that the hand would regain any semblance of function?

I worked my way down the ladder and boarded *SAKAMO*. Engine down, motor engaged, fenders stowed, lines released, I pushed the throttle forward and pointed toward Portland as the sun rose over Peaks Island, bathing the distant waterfront in a buttery glow.

The direct flight to Pittsburgh took an hour and a half. An impenetrable fog hung over the city. After paying the taxi fare, I made my way up a steep hill toward my destination, passing Jewish and Middle Eastern delicatessens, Chinese restaurants, and butcher shops. It was as if I'd entered an entirely different dimension through an ocean portal. I stopped in front of the Presbyterian University Medical Center, and noted that my community hospital could easily fit inside the ground floor.

Upstairs, I shook hands with Dr. Medsger, the department chair, and with the faculty seated around the conference table. One physician in an immaculate white coat and crisp bow-tie noted that the program had never interviewed an osteopathic physician before. I took that as a compliment, and said that I viewed my experience in primary care as a solid foundation to build on. A Dr. Wasko looked up from reviewing my application. "I thought your internal medicine residency was at a small community hospital? How did you arrange for rotations at New England Medical Center, Yale New Haven Hospital, and the Cleveland Clinic?"

"Because the Osteopathic Hospital of Maine has a limited specialty medical staff, the head of my residency suggested that I apply for elective months at some of the larger medical centers to round out my training. I wrote letters to the program directors and followed that up with a phone call. Well, several phone calls. It seemed to work, particularly for my rheumatology electives."

After a tour of the hospital and a brief walk around the University of Pittsburgh campus, I caught a taxi back to the airport. I must have been a puzzle to them; a primary care DO with experience in immunology and rheumatology. A moment before the taxi disappeared into the Fort Pitt tunnel, I turned and looked back at the Pittsburgh skyline. The outlines of a sailboat emerged out of the mist on the Allegheny River. Dark clouds obscured the low-lying mountains and all but the lower floors of the downtown office buildings. I might as well have been looking out from Peaks Island toward Portland on a gray, fog-bound morning.

That night, as Sandi and I settled into bed, she asked, "What was Pittsburgh like?"

"I don't know," I answered. "I arrived in the fog and departed in the fog. The interview went . . . I don't know, fairly well."

"Well, they wouldn't have interviewed you if they didn't think you were a good candidate. I'm glad you're home." Sandi closed her book and turned off the light.

It had been six weeks since the nuns departed Peaks Island. The Saint Joseph's by the Sea nunnery was now the Mother of the Good Shepherd Monastery, where Father Seamus and his seeing-eye dog, Brendon, and Brother Nicholas lived. Clinic was not the same without Sister Mia. She made poor choices in the quantity of food she ingested. The woman had a temper. But disclose a confidence requiring empathy, compassion, and faith, and she hung on like a bulldog, even if her body was held together by baling wire. I missed her. The monks were remarkably healthy. I had yet to meet them for a clinic visit. Their first samples of beer were rumored to be quite tasty.

Yesterday, Sandi boarded the *Machigonne* and took a seat on the bench below deck across from Father Seamus and Brother Nicholas. Immediately next to her was an unfamiliar man in a long chestnut-colored robe and a coal-black, ragged beard. It was a blustery day, and when the ferry churned out of the inner harbor, it plowed through southwest swells rolling in from the open ocean. Abruptly, the *Machigonne* lost power. Broadside against the waves, the ferry wallowed side to side. Two crewmen raced down the stairs and disappeared into the engine room. A few minutes later, one of the crew emerged and announced, "We've temporarily lost steerage; no worries, we'll be fine."

The new monk leaned forward, rocking, his eyes darting up and down the aisle, his face emptying out into a pasty mask. He ran a sweaty hand through a shock of greasy hair. Abruptly, he turned to Sandi and said, "This really sucks." Sandi blinked her eyes in disbelief. A few minutes later the engine came online and the ferry made a broad, slow turn, limping back to Portland on one engine.

The monk, it's rumored, disembarked on the Portland side, never to be seen again.

My first patient at clinic this morning was Lois Herndon. I watched from my desk as she stepped lively through the entrance and chatted with Anne at the check-in counter before taking a seat next to the toy bin. A toddler dropped a ball and it rolled under Lois's seat. Without hesitation, Lois squatted down and reached under the chair and retrieved the ball. This feat of dexterity was proof that her rib fractures were fully healed. It had been months since I'd discontinued her last milligram of prednisone. Like so many others on long-term prednisone, Lois struggled with weight gain, diabetes, mood changes, and osteoporosis. I recently came across a mistyped medical transcription report I'd dictated last winter summarizing Lois's side-effects: *Patient's prednisone curse (course) is complete.*

Her visit today was for a "tune-up" for chronic neck and low-back pain. She lay on her back on the exam table as I palpated the paraspinal muscles for signs of local tenderness or restricted motion. Where there was restriction, I pressed more firmly on the affected muscle group, rotated and side-bent it into a position of comfort, and held this position until I felt the muscle relax. With her history of osteoporosis, this was no time to forcibly manipulate her spine.

Every two weeks for the past several months, at the conclusion of each session, Lois had requested a follow-up. Who was I to decide when she'd reached maximum improvement? For my part, the soft tissue manipulation was a pleasant interlude in an otherwise hectic day. My mind drifted as I moved from the base of her skull, through the cervical and thoracic muscles, into the bulky lumbar muscle groups. Although I was not as skilled in the art of manipulation as many of my DO peers, I was convinced that the laying on of hands had therapeutic value, and, as I cradled her neck in my hands, I was reminded of a quote attributed to A.T. Still, the founder of osteopathic medicine: *To find health should be the object of the doctor. Anyone can find disease.*

At the conclusion of the visit, Lois claimed I purposefully left one last muscle with residual discomfort to ensure her return. At the door, I turned and smiled, "I can cure your back pain, but then we may not have anything to talk about."

Scribbling a note in her chart on my way to my desk, I passed Mr. Slater as he lumbered onto the hallway scale. "296 pounds," Anne quietly announced.

"Good God!" Mr. Slater said, "This is the first time in a year that I've dropped under 300 pounds. No wonder I'm feeling lighter on my feet. Here, I've written a list of my medications along with the current doses." He handed it to Anne as she led him into the exam room. "At my visit with the cardiologist yesterday, she made a minor adjustment in my diuretic dose. I must say, she's moving the medications around like pieces on a chess board."

I opened Mr. Slater's chart and paused for a moment at the door while Anne settled him into the exam room, dialing down my expectations. I suspected that Mr. Slater's unhealthy habits and habitus were decades old, perhaps lifelong. The fact that he underwent gastric bypass surgery and gained back the weight—and then some—often pointed to deep-seated underlying emotional trauma. While it was possible to be both overweight and healthy, those who are morbidly obese (greater than 100 pounds over ideal body weight) could be a challenging subgroup to work with.

If they smoke, they are the patients who often gain weight with attempts to quit. If they are depressed, the medications necessary to manage their depression contribute to further weight gain. What's more, once patients are morbidly obese, they often develop arthritis in the hips or knees, making exercise difficult, if not impossible. Even if they cut back on calories, the ability to burn calories is severely limited. The result: massively overweight patients often boxed in by their emotional illnesses and co-morbidities.

Entering the room, I extended my hand. "Your last visit, when you were short of breath and I called the fireboat, weren't you wearing a black T-shirt with the slogan, *Chess, Where the Elite Meet?*"

"That was no accident. I'm a Class B, category 2 player on the Elo scale."

"I see. That must require considerable practice and concentration."

"Indeed, it does." Mr. Slater relaxed into his chair. I glanced at his ankles; his swelling was markedly improved. "If you must know, I think most clearly when I snack during a match. Of course, I also find myself snacking when I visualize a match. And I play and visualize constantly; it's an obsession, really. The satisfaction of a well-played game comes with the cost of a gluttonous meal. The two are inexplicably linked."

There, a confession of sorts. I rested my hand on my chin and curled a finger around my lower lip. On one level, Mr. Slater's visit was focused on hypertension, diabetes, congestive heart failure, sleep apnea, and arthritis. And of course, adjusting this and that medication might achieve some benefit, perhaps keeping him out of the hospital, which was not a minor miracle. But I was intrigued. Was it possible to sever the link between Mr. Slater's love of chess and his insatiable urge to overeat? As we sat quietly staring at the space between us, it was clear it was my move.

"I'm sure you've tried to substitute lower calorie snacks during a match? Say, carrots or celery?" I asked.

"Of course. That was an abysmal failure."

"Right. I'm not surprised. Diabetic foods? Low-calorie snacks meant to imitate a hearty desert?"

"Have you ever tasted one of those abominations?"

"No," I answered.

"Well, you might try a package sometime. I would rather chew on a tablecloth."

"True," I conceded. "Smaller portions? More thorough chewing?"

After a moment he said, "I worked with a psychotherapist for a number of years. Very interesting. But in the end, a more intimate understanding of my psyche did little to uncouple my lust for food."

Checkmate. He shrugged his shoulders. I silently opened his chart, pivoting my mind toward more mundane matters of abnormal lab and medication adjustments. A little extra insulin here. An increased dose of blood pressure medication there. "Hypnotism?" I wondered out loud. "Have you ever undergone hypnotism?"

"Of course not. It's all mumbo jumbo to me." Then Mr. Slater leaned forward and wondered, "It *is* a bunch of mumbo jumbo, is it not?"

"That's hard to say," I said. "I know a psychologist in Portland who offers hypnotism as an adjunct for his patients. Apparently, it comprises a significant portion of his practice. A patient of mine believes the hypnosis sessions helped her quit smoking after she'd failed everything else. Your problem is more complex, but you never know. Here," I reached into a drawer and handed Mr. Slater the psychologist's card. "Think it over. In the meantime, let's increase your long-acting insulin by ten units in the morning and by five units in the late afternoon. Oh, and bump up your metoprolol by fifty milligrams at bedtime, that should smooth out your morning blood pressure readings." I wrote down the instructions and made an appointment for two weeks.

Mr. Slater rose, still eyeing the card, and placed it in his wallet. Tipping his hat, he turned and in a quiet, almost inaudible voice said, "I appreciate your interest. Thank you for your insight. I believe the next move is up to me."

Then there was Dan, my patient with a solidly entrenched phobia for solid foods. In the past year, he'd made progress with select soft foods, but still suffered nightmares about his car accident years ago, when he'd choked on a sausage sandwich after plowing into a truck. His wife Sarah, who accompanied him on all of his appointments, was grateful that his weight was up fifteen pounds in the last six months. I flipped through his chart and located his psychiatrist's recent note. The combination of amitriptyline at night and clonazepam during the day had led to fewer panic attacks. Sarah wondered if smoking marijuana had helped.

Dan is more upbeat than I'd seen him in years. He was taking long walks through the interior of the island, where he cut and pulled invasive bittersweet vines. He'd joined the Peaks Island Land Preserve and was valued for his efforts to restore some of the island's natural balance now that the deer herd had been dramatically thinned.

I glanced at my watch: *SAKAMO* was temporarily out of the water due to a clogged fuel line. Twenty minutes until the next ferry. It would be close. Anne handed me the chart of my last patient: Johnny Dinsmore. Oh my.

Johnny looked up as I entered the room. He rolled up his sleeves and removed his shoes and socks. I braced myself for disaster. His hands and feet were normal. With growing astonishment, I pulled up his pants legs and the knees looked . . . normal. Abruptly, the diminutive Irishman jumped up and danced an awkward jig, singing a tune vaguely reminiscent of *My Wild Irish Rose* with the line, "I have searched everywhere but none is now there, my gout be gone, gone, gone." Outside the door, Anne howled. Johnny was not my first singing patient, but the event was an unexpected joy. When he was done, I slapped him on the back and encouraged him to stay with the daily allopurinol; that was the key.

"That, and the black cherries!" Johnny corrected me. "Don't forget the cherries!"

"Yes, of course, the black cherries," I echoed. "But remember, the cherries will lose their power if you discontinue the allopurinol. Let's make sure you have a year of refills on the allopurinol." I handed him the prescription, scribbled a quick note and was on my bike to the ferry landing with four minutes remaining before the *Machigonne* pushed off.

Hanging a right at the candy store, I raced down Welch Street as the crew undid the lines to the gangplank. By the time I parked the bike and gathered my backpack, the *Machigonne* was backing off the wharf. I sheepishly held my green satchel aloft and pleaded for a ride to town. My antics caught the eye of the captain, who in a moment of weakness, reversed engines and allowed me to board.

Peering out the window from inside the hold, I noticed the Quinbys' dive boat pulling a heavily loaded barge off Little Diamond Island. It was moving day. I took the ferry stairs two at a time and stood on the upper deck, flapping my arms, hoping Dave might glance in my direction.

From inside the pilot house, Dave opened the port window and shouted in my direction, "It's exactly one-hundred miles to Isle au Haut! Come see us for a house-call sometime!" On the bow of the dive boat, Marsha and the Quinby children sat on sea urchin crates. In the center of the barge, a load of furniture was lashed together. A flock of gulls, attracted by the smell of sea urchins and formaldehyde, circled overhead. I waved to the Quinbys and shook off the sadness I knew would inevitably come.

In my green satchel was a letter of acceptance to the University of Pittsburgh's fellowship in rheumatology and clinical immunology. Sandi had reluctantly taken the moving boxes out of the attic. She did not completely embrace our upcoming move, but was keeping an open mind.

There was reason for optimism. Life might actually be simpler in Pittsburgh. We'd put down a deposit on a rented house in a quiet neighborhood within walking distance of the hospital. There was a nearby zoo and a large urban park. During our recent visit to the park, Sandi had spotted rabbits and squirrels, two species that didn't exist on Peaks Island. We gaped at them as if they were exotic, endangered species.

Sandi had located a preschool for Molly, with a playground. Kate would attend second grade at Colfax Grammar School. With nearly a thousand students, it would be her first experience as a minority among Black, Asian, and Hispanic students. At our visit to Colfax, the Black assistant principal did a double take when she spied Kate. With obvious affection, she wrapped an arm around Kate and embraced her in a bear hug. "Your daughter is the spitting image of my little sister!" If only we all could be so color blind.

Our house on Peaks Island was rented for the next two years. Now that our bathroom interior pipes were wrapped with heat tape, Sandi didn't know how they could possibly freeze, but I'd heard that before. Just in case, she'd left our renters detailed instructions on the use of a blow dryer.

Off House Island, I watched a deer emerge from the underbrush at the top of the gravel beach. The buck peered up and down the channel before it waded into the water and swam effortlessly toward Peaks Island. The wake gently rocked Bobby Emerson's lobster boat, and Bobby looked up from baiting a trap and silently followed the deer's progress across the channel. Reaching shore, the deer shook itself off and bounded into the woods. By nightfall, I was certain that Bobby would know exactly where the buck had bedded down.

My practice was in good hands. Lisa Rudenberg, a family practice osteopathic physician, had agreed to assume my clinic duties on Peaks Island. It was a perfect fit; with three children under the age of seven, she wanted to work part-time. And she had some experience with the islands. When she was a medical student, she accompanied me on several house calls, including a visit to Cliff Island to see an 80-year-old woman who longed for pierced ears. It was the first and only time that I'd combined a hypertension and diabetes check-up with ear piercing. The patient wept. Of all the house calls I performed on the islands, the pierced ears—complete with ear studs—was, without a doubt, my favorite.

As an added bonus, Lisa's husband, Dan Merson, a DO internist, was picking up my Portland practice. Dan, who had performed my treadmill when the health of my heart was uncertain, was a good fit for the practice. He'd already experienced his share of stubborn patients— namely, me. He wanted to build a boat, which boded well for keeping Lisa and their growing family engaged with the islands.

And yet, I worried. Despite my attraction to rheumatology, was I making the wrong choice? Sandi, to her credit, pointed out that I was not running away from general medicine, but toward a branch of medicine I'd felt an attraction for since my college days. How else could I explain that, despite my grueling schedule, I'd made time these past five years for the weekly rheumatology conference at Maine Medical Center. When we returned, I'd be better equipped to take care of Ben Shipman's rheumatoid arthritis and Lois Herndon's giant cell arteritis (unfortunately, her vasculitis can relapse). The young girl with lupus might return to my care.

The pace of change in medicine was accelerating. Perhaps, during my practice life-time, cures for autoimmune diseases would be developed. Someday, prednisone would be viewed as a relic of the twentieth century, a treatment that saved lives but with side effects nearly as devastating as the disease itself. I wanted to see that day.

I located the truck keys in my front pocket and my wallet in the back left. On the bottom of my backpack, double-wrapped in a Tupperware container, were lab slips and samples of Lois Herndon's and Johnny Dinsmore's blood. In a side compartment were two apples, a Snickers bar, and a stack of unfinished charts. I had an uneasy feeling. There was something else. There was always something else. Then it came to me. I pulled out my pocket calendar and wrote: *House call tonight, Ruth.* On the opposite page was a quote I'd recently written down from Dr. William Osler on the practice of medicine: *As physicians we should strive to cure a few, help most, but comfort all."* Its as true today as it was more than a hundred years ago. Tonight, I'd bring Kate and Molly along for Ruth's house call. Together, we'd see what we could do.